Dear ♥ Child

Four Journeys

to

Successful Open Adoption

Sydney, Elle, Ginger, and Julia

With Constance Skedgell

Published by BEXSI Publishing, LLC

www.AuthorYourBrand.com

The opinions expressed by the author are not necessarily those of
Bexsi Publishing, LLC.

This book is designed to provide accurate and authoritative
information with regard to the subject matter covered. This
information is given with the understanding that neither the
author nor Bexsi Publishing, LLC, is engaged in rendering legal
or professional advice. Since the details of your situation are fact
dependent, you should additionally seek the services of a competent
professional.

ISBN-13: 978-0-9914939-2-0 (paperback)

ISBN-13: 978-0-9844561-9-2 (cloth)

Printed in USA by Bexsi Publishing

Contents

Dear Child......

"Child of the world: into my heart you came, bringing sun into my life, making family our name."

Dedications

Cole, you fill our life, home, and our family with so much joy. You are worth all the heartbreak of waiting. Everyone said a baby would find us, and we are so grateful you were placed in our life. I wrote this book to share with you, and so many others waiting to find their baby, the hope that you and they would see the beauty and blessings adoption can bring. You have our whole heart for our whole life. We love you more than one single word can describe.

Peace, love, and gratitude.

Mommy

(Sydney)

I give this book with love to you, Harper. I love you more than words can express, baby. I hope that through this book, you can literally see and feel the love your Daddy and I have for you. You are our greatest joy in life and undoubtedly the greatest gift we will ever be given. Ever. You did not come to me through my body, but through my heart.

I am Forever Yours,

Mommy

(Elle)

This book is dedicated to the three most important men in my life.

To my son, Benjamin: You have filled my heart with more joy in the year I have known you than I could have imagined. I love you more than the words in this book could ever describe.

To my husband, Oscar: You are my rock. Thank you for never wavering in your devotion on this journey. I love parenting by your side, being your best friend, and being your lover. I'm yours.

To my savior, Jesus: I am humbled and grateful every time I look at my son. You sustain and pursue me through good times and bad. You have never forgotten your promise, giving me more than I ever deserved. Until we meet face to face, may my heart sing praise to you.

Love,

Momma

(Julia)

I dedicate this book to many people. To my family for giving me the support I needed to pursue adoption. To Gordon for helping me find balance. To my son, Ethan, who introduced me to the incredible bond between mother and child. And to my daughter, Olivia: we finally found each other! And you were worth every step of the journey!

Love,

Mommy

(Ginger)

Dear Reader,

We are four friends who found our babies through adoption. In this book, each adoptive mother describes to you, in her own honest and heartfelt words, an adoption journey that was startlingly different from the others.

Three of us live in California, one in Colorado. We started trying to make families in our mid-thirties and, in one case, early forties. One of the four already had a child through a donor egg. We're all married, with professional backgrounds. None of us ever dreamed we would adopt.

The paths that led us to embrace adopting, and our adoption journeys themselves, were filled with drama and emotion. Along the way, we experienced the lowest lows and the highest highs of our lives.

Out of our many conversations with one another about those wildly zigzagging emotions, this book was conceived. We shared so many feelings and reactions unique to this situation. At the same time, we marveled at how *different* our fertility and adoption journeys had been. And we never stopped being amazed that, for all four of us friends, adoption turned out to be the answer.

The diversity of our adoption experiences, coupled with our friendships, seemed unusual to us—remarkable. It occurred to two of us that, almost at the same moment, other people might be interested in our interlocking stories… *a book!* As soon as the word was articulated, the universe seemed to smile. Yes, a book! The book would be a record of our amazing experiences; it would be a source of inspiration and information for others; and it would be a loving gift to our children when the time was right.

But what kind of book? We knew we wanted the focus to be on our feelings. There are enough factual how-to guides to adopting out there. We didn't see the point in adding one more to the flood. And, anyway, that wasn't where our hearts were. We wanted to describe our journeys with such raw honesty that you, our reader, could feel with us, every step of the way. This would be the inside story of adoption: how it feels, moment by moment. We also decided to write from a female point of view, so that the book would be by and primarily about us, the adoptive moms. (Dads, both biological and adoptive, grab the spotlight in chapter six.) This decision felt right: we wanted to tell *our* stories and give words to *our* feelings. Our wonderfully supportive husbands said, "Go for it!" (We suspect they were relieved to get out of writing!)

However, we four are not professional writers. We needed to involve someone who could edit our outpourings, structure the mass of material, and add some writing to weave the stories together. That person needed to "get it"... to be moved and excited by the idea of the book. One of the journey moms found that person in Constance, a freelance writer and editor whom she'd worked with years earlier. Constance was totally on board with the idea that we four moms would write about our adoption journeys, each in our own way, flavored by our personalities, and that as editor, she would preserve those differences.

Integral to all our journeys was the fact that we opted for *open* adoption. In open adoption, as opposed to traditional, "closed" adoption, birth parents and adoptive parents know one another's identities and exchange contact information that lets them stay in touch. The birth mother has sole discretion in picking the adoptive parents (sometimes with the involvement of the birth father)—thus, the overwhelming importance of winning her heart through the "birth mom letter," which you'll read about in chapter three. Post-adoption, birth parents continue to have contact with the adoptive family as agreed upon in degree and manner.

It's interesting to us that, according to a 2012 study, currently about 55 percent of American adoptions are fully open, with ongoing contact that includes the child. Another 40 percent are "mediated adoptions," in which the adoption agency facilitates periodic exchanges of pictures and letters, but typically no direct contact. Contrast that with just twenty years ago, when 1 percent of domestic adoptions were open.

The same study shows that when those involved choose some form of open adoption, adoptive families are happier with the process, birth mothers experience less regret and worry, and adopted children benefit from having access to their birth relatives, as well as to their family and medical histories.

Well, we can't say we're surprised by all these positive findings about open adoption!

Our book is not meant to be an advertisement for going the route of open adoption. However, this choice has shaped our experiences, and much that you will read in these pages deals with the interplay of relationships resulting from those choices. Despite the fact that the sweet promise of open adoption has not always worked out as we'd hoped, we four know it is the right choice for us. Is it best for everyone? We're not comfortable making a blanket statement here. This book might help you decide for yourself by offering a no-holes-barred perspective from four insiders.

If you are contemplating adoption, or if you have adopted, we hope our book inspires you on *your* journey, and shows you the indescribable happiness that is within reach.

Chapter ♡ One
Tick-Tock

After crayoning and reading The Cat in the Hat *in her son's kindergarten class, red-haired Ginger throws on a suit after lunch for a series of high-stakes sales calls in the San Francisco area. Mom to Ethan and his pert-faced little sister, Olivia, Ginger's ideal day includes a yoga class with her mom. (Yeah, she actually adores being with family.) Working from home with her attorney husband, conference calls are balanced by pillow fights, peanut butter sandwiches, and bear hugs for both kids.*

Ginger

I remember having an ultrasound and my doctor telling me my ovaries did not look very "juicy." What am I, a dried-up raisin? I was only thirty-two.

From age thirty-one to thirty-nine, having a baby was the number one focus of my life. Looking back now, I realize how much time, effort, money, and marital strife went into the process.

Collectively, I had dozens of intrauterine inseminations (IUIs) and nine in vitro fertilization (IVF) procedures (six fresh, three frozen). My husband and I were lucky enough to become parents of Ethan through the miracle of donor eggs, and this made it possible for me to let go of the need for a biological connection with my child. Actually, that part was easy. It would have been nice to see what my husband and I would have created, but with my bunions and über-fair skin, I was okay with using another woman's eggs. Almost immediately after my son was born, I was back to my baby-making hobby with more IVF. I only breast-fed Ethan for four months so I could get my body back on track to make another. I was obviously not thinking clearly. I did not allow myself a chance to enjoy the moment.

Having one child only made me want another. My entire emotional world was riding on details of a cycle—how many eggs, how many were fertilized, how thick my uterine lining was.

And then the two-week wait: the period between the transfer of embryos and the results. I had always heard, "You cannot be a little bit pregnant." But that is wrong. You can be a little bit pregnant when an embryo is dropped into your uterus, and you hope every day the embryo implants and grows... visualizing a healthy lining for nourishing the tiny bean... doing acupuncture... shots and oral meds... taking herbs and eating a diet devoid of caffeine, alcohol, wheat, dairy, and sugar... walking lightly so as not to rattle anything inside the delicate warming hut of life.

It's hard for me to imagine anything worse than putting all you have into a cycle and getting a call from a very sweet nurse saying, "I don't have good news for you," or, even worse, a weak positive and you have to stay on the shots and pray. I had put so much pressure on myself, on my body, on modern medicine, to make me happy.

April 9, 2009, is a significant date for me. On that day, I lost a baby at fifteen weeks. Like so many who miscarry, I blamed myself. But, for me, it was different.

I had traveled to a mountain resort, and knew the high altitude had caused the miscarriage. It was my fault. I was responsible for this tiny lost life. How could I have let this happen? All the money, time, and effort on a donor IVF cycle... and I blew it.

My three-year-old son would not have a sibling, my family would not be complete, and I would have to live with it. I had a recurring nightmare that I was being prosecuted in a court of law because I had killed the baby inside of me. This was a dark period in my otherwise very happy life. I had dealt with other fertility challenges—a ruptured ectopic that resulted in the loss of both tubes, several failed/negative IVFs, a couple of earlier termed miscarriages—but I was not prepared for this type of pain.

My husband, sister, mom, and best friend, Kiki, saw me at my worst. And there was nothing they could really do to fix it. The sad reality is I was truly alone in this process, even with people around who were trying to love and support me.

I did not want to feel better; I felt like I did not deserve it. But I had a three-year-old son, a husband, and a job, all of which needed attention. I owed it to these commitments and to myself to get better. I needed to fix it. And I did. I filled the void. I knew a second child was right for our family. I was done with IVF.

Adoption was the way.

For sweet-faced Julia, who met her husband doing mission work across the world, fertility struggles were complicated by devastating illness. An architect, she now lives with husband Oscar and their rosy-cheeked son, Benjamin, in a cozy bungalow in Colorado. Julia has had her share of challenges, and is strengthened by her faith. As soon as she took the first step on the path to adoption, she felt a sweeping relief. The endless struggle with forces beyond her control was over. She could move forward with hope.

Julia

It was six long years before my husband and I started the process of adoption. We struggled through vasectomy reversal, fertility treatments, IVF, and the final blow: I had a stroke in 2009. The recovery from that was long and arduous, and really set back my plan to have a baby. I didn't even know if I could get pregnant, or if it was even safe.

Because of my faith, I struggled with the question of why I worked so hard to have my own children when I knew there were children out there who desperately needed parents. I knew God loves adoption and maybe that was what He wanted for my life and for the life of some precious child. It was an internal conflict between Him and me. How did He feel about me working so hard to control this aspect of my life? Maybe He had something better out there for me, yet I was digging in my heels, fighting against it.

Two years after I had the stroke, I had almost completely recovered. I began the baby pursuit again and started talking with my husband, Oscar, about our options. For some reason, the idea of trying IVF again was terrifying. I didn't know if I could take the emotional roller coaster again (little did I know that the journey of adoption would have its own ride). Oscar, however, really wanted us to have our own biological children and seemed set on that course.

Oscar is twenty-five years older than me, so *his* clock was ticking faster than mine. In a sense, it was done. Though he has three sons from a previous marriage, he was dedicated to having a family with me. We'd been married for only two years when we decided to start building our family; however, both of us were still having fun with our freedom, without kids. We enjoyed travelling extensively, going out when we wanted, and just enjoying each other, one on one. It was ultimately my clock that went off. With each year that passed, more and more of my friends and family members were having babies and building their families, and I began to realize how desperately I wanted the same. I think the pain of infertility also made the desire for a child grow stronger.

Oscar and I initially tried the old-fashioned way to have children. We knew it would be difficult. I had had a history of significant endometriosis. He'd had a vasectomy. Once we confirmed through testing that there was a *chance* I could get pregnant naturally, Oscar had a reversal. But we struggled for the next year. We began fertility treatments. After two unsuccessful rounds of intrauterine insemination (IUI), we decided to try IVF.

Through IVF, I actually got pregnant, only to miscarry after ten weeks. It was heartbreaking. I didn't know how I could have come that far only to miscarry. I was angry and depressed. I didn't know how God could let this happen to me, and I sunk into depression.

At that point, Oscar challenged me to ask God for a promise—a passage of Scripture. God immediately led me to Psalm 113. The very last verse says, "He settles the childless women in her home as a happy mother." I am not a "well-Bibled" Christian, so when He led me to this uniquely suitable verse, I believed it was His promise to me. I didn't know how that would play out in my life, but I knew and trusted it would.

It was during our annual Thanksgiving trip to Oscar's parents' home in California (we live in Colorado) that we began to seriously consider adoption. We had met our friends, Phillip and Sydney, one year before. For some reason—and now I know it was meant to be, and why—we really connected. We learned of each other's fertility challenges, and Sydney and I began to deeply connect on that journey.

That year—our second meeting—we met their adopted son, Cole. And Sydney and Phillip shared intimate details of their adoption story with us. We identified with their pain and desire, and now saw their precious baby boy. Their positive story really encouraged Oscar. And that really encouraged *me*!

I think I had always had a heart for adoption, yet I also wanted to have biological children. Before our infertility struggles, it never occurred to me that I wouldn't be able to. Adoption was just a nice option that was out there. But when faced with the fact that I probably couldn't have babies, adoption showed up on my radar. I had mixed emotions—feeling excited about finally having a family, yet fearing the appearance of failure. (What was wrong with me? With my husband? With my marriage?)

We spent about a month thinking about adoption, and gave ourselves a January 1 deadline to decide which (if any) path to take toward a child. I remember waking up on New Year's morning and lying in bed with my husband talking about it. On January 2, I began calling adoption agencies. That was the day I was all in.

Dear ♡ Child

Once a personal shopper for John F. Kennedy, Jr., and owner of her own retail boutique, Elle still helps a devoted clientele of ladies find that "perfect" outfit. In her Marin County, California, home, she's created a poppin' fuschia-and-white kiddie corner for one special little lady: dark-haired, pouty-lipped Harper. For Elle, too, adoption offered a welcome feeling of taking charge of her life.

Elle

When my husband, Jack, and I first talked about beginning a family, we thought I would get pregnant easily. I wanted to go through the pregnancy experience, and I always wondered what a child would be like with our combined genes. People always joked that we'd have Olympic athletes, as Jack is 6'4" and athletic and I am 5'6" and athletic. So I guess those two reasons are why I tried to get pregnant for so long. Our plan was to adopt our second child, and give love and a great life to a child in need of a family.

From the very beginning, Jack and I were wide open to adoption. Both he and I come from divorced and not so "perfect" family situations, and knew that *true* family isn't limited to who gave birth to you. Jack's stepfather adopted him as an infant, then his bipolar mom officially went looney and left him and his brothers motherless when Jack was at the ripe old age of fourteen, during his freshman year of high school... ouch. How's that for an opener?

Eventually, when it was clear—after years of trying to conceive with all the big guns loaded (and reloaded way too many times) via numerous rounds of Clomid, IUI, IVF, acupuncture, and three minor surgeries to get the ole' reproductive system "open for business"—that a baby was not going to come through my body physically, ever, we both readily decided to skip our planned "one baby coming naturally" phase and make our adopted "second child" our first. I now hate to use that word "naturally," because our adopted baby girl, Harper, *is* our "natural" daughter. She is OUR baby, 100 percent… our firstborn who was just not "physically carried by me."

So I guess you could say the exact moment I decided to give up having a baby physically and began to find our "adopted baby"—whom I knew was out there somewhere in the universe—was after our third and final IVF attempt. Jack and I agreed it would be our last try via IVF because of the mounting costs. We were in over $75,000 with nothing to show for it but our maxed-out credit cards during the worst of the 2008 economic shake-up, my struggling business, and the loss of all my hopes for "carrying" a baby.

I also was so over living my life around IVF attempts—you can't drink, work out, be stressed-out, and have sex at certain times (and then, when you do have sex, you feel like you have a gun to your head). You could almost say I was a human voodoo doll—but, instead of someone stabbing me with pins, I was stabbing myself with the biggest needles you've ever seen, filled with "magic potions" to get me knocked up. I was giving myself my own injections in the ass and abdomen three times a day with a 25-gauge needle that was—excuse my French—goddamn big. Literally, your life is on an extended pause; you are in a marathon of time, money, and emotion. And guess what? There are no guarantees that a baby will be at the finish line to meet you, which is a HUGE letdown both physically and mentally.

That final, empty, "nobody understands how heartbroken I feel… can I please just curl up in a cave and die" moment that nailed the coffin shut for me came when I was in Los Angeles on a work trip for Fashion Week. (At the time, I was the owner/head buyer of a women's boutique.) It was two weeks after the transfer had taken place, and I was going to see if one of the three embryos had taken. Secretly, I was hoping that two took, because I had always dreamt of having two kids. And, now, with all the problems of getting pregnant, I thought this would be a blessing.

I remember going into the lab at seven a.m. and telling myself that if this didn't work out, I was never going into a lab and getting blood drawn to see if "it" took ever again. Period. When I was informed later that day, in the middle of fashion meetings, that the test was negative, I knew I would be taking a completely new path.

I threw myself deeply into the rest of my market appointments that day so I could escape the hurt for a few hours. Emotionally, I was numb. That night, when I got back to my married-with-children friend's house where I was staying for the week, I remember smiling and telling everyone I was "totally okay… no biggie…" As I said this, my heart was pounding in my throat and I know they thought I was full of it. They were so right. What made it even harder was they were saying, "Don't worry; you *will* have a baby," as I played with their three kids. I might also add that my friend was only thirty-four and was toying with just popping out another. Bitch.

When I got back home to San Francisco, Jack and I had a follow-up with my IVF doctor. As she walked us through different explanations for why the three IVF attempts all came up a bust, it became obvious Renée had no answers for us. This just frustrated me even more. The meeting ended with Renée suggesting the surrogate route, which I always thought was *so* absurd. But now, all of a sudden, in the desperate place I was at, having another woman carry my baby didn't seem so nuts after all. That was the last time I spoke to Renée. She had been at the center of my universe for three years; now I was beyond done with her.

Jack and I decided to go the surrogate route, and I chose a doctor. After a cool conference call with him, and a huge packet sent to us from his office, I was ready to attempt the impossible feat once again but in another woman's body this time.

On the phone, I went over the protocol with a nurse: the injections and what I'd be doing to get ready for this literal "out-of-body experience." But my positive state of mind about the surrogate path came to an immediate halt when I heard the nurse's last words to me: "Call us back once you find your surrogate." *Oh, damn, now I have to go find a surrogate.*

I was done. Adoption, here we come, charging down your path.

Once I made the appointment to go to our first "meeting," which would start the adoption process, I instantly felt in control. For four years I had been riding in the back seat. Now I was in the driver's seat… and it felt SO DAMN GREAT!

Blonde and casually chic, she was a major player at a pioneering mineral makeup company, also guiding a hot online beauty company to off-the-charts success. Sydney shops for deals and steals, and takes long "urban hikes" with her dreamy-eyed son, Cole. The family's giant picture window overlooks San Francisco Bay. It's a beautiful new beginning... exactly what adoption offered.

Sydney

I will never forget the day my husband and I decided that adoption was the path for us. I was excited, scared, and baffled by the process, yet incredibly motivated by the prospect of bringing a child into our home and starting the next chapter of our marriage as a family.

We'd just gone through an exhausting year trying alternative methods of getting pregnant. We'd been through five IVF transfers with our surrogate, and we were at the end of our embryos. I had decided that, once we exhausted all our embryos, we would change course. But let me flash back for a minute...

After years of building a great career in the beauty industry, but zigzagging as I chased the dream of marriage and kids, I realized I was waiting for one thing: Phillip. We met in our twenties and married in our forties, with a lot of back and forth in each other's lives for over fifteen years. We were both busy building our careers and growing independently, but we finally decided we wanted to share with each other what we'd each created over the years. Our favorite saying was "worth the wait"—like a fine wine, it's best to drink it when it's ready!

When we finally woke up to the "happily ever after," it was starting a family that turned out to be our greatest challenge in our life together. Yikes! I was forty-two with nothing but fertility issues; Phillip, at forty-five, was wondering about the same thing for the first time. From fibroids that had taken over my uterus at the young age of twenty-seven, to aging eggs, I didn't stand a chance. But I was comforted knowing we had the means to go after alternative methods. And, determined to make it happen, I set out to do so.

My business mind loves a challenge and forming a plan that leads to a solution. I handled our personal situation in the same way. I threw myself into finding the solution, knowing the problem all tied back to me. After heartfelt conversations and "business planning" together, I convinced Phillip that all we needed was someone to carry our embryo. Simple! But "carrying our embryo" sounded easier than it was. A real, live baby ended up being *two times* removed from me—a nearly forty-four-year-old woman with no usable uterus or eggs! Outsourcing now became a matter of finding both an egg donor and surrogate. Phillip liked to describe the process as "shopping in a catalog."

After a while, we got really comfortable telling people we were "outsourcing." However, the next year was not easy. We went through a series of exhausting, emotional, heart-connecting experiences with our surrogate and her family. Our IVF transfers led to two positive but not full-term pregnancies. The best IVF doctor in the San Francisco Bay Area encouraged us during the entire process, telling us we had "all the right pieces in place" for a positive pregnancy. It all looked good on paper, so we tried and tried until we exhausted the resource. When we ran out of embryos, that was the end for me. *It was such a relief to now finally have a line in the sand.*

It was hard to let down my surrogate, who was so emotionally attached to doing this for us. But I am not one to keep failing when there are alternative routes. Adoption was next on our list. Actually, Phillip had wanted to adopt even before we went the surrogate route. But I'd begged him to let us try with a surrogate first. Now I was so happy to have it all be over.

At last, I didn't have to think twice about our next step. I just had to pick up the phone and schedule a meeting with an adoption attorney. Everything was full speed ahead from that moment on.

I realize now how much I took for granted as I moved into adulthood. I had thought at one time that once you get married, you just naturally start to procreate and that, within months, you got pregnant. I am left very humbled. During the years I was dreaming of being married with kids, I once said I would never adopt.

I was so young and naïve. I feel fortunate to be wise enough later in life to open my mind to the astonishing world of adoption. It took us less than six months from start to finish, and we received the best gift in our life, our son. Cole was the biggest blessing for all the work we did to get there. "Worth the wait" read our adoption announcement.

When Sydney, Julia, Elle, and Ginger made the decision to adopt, some of their husbands backed the choice from the start. Others needed to warm up to the idea. While Ginger's husband was open to adoption, he wanted to move slowly into this unknown territory. Not Ginger. She was so ready. She was sprinting.

Ginger

After my miscarriage, I realized my body was not cooperating and that I was at the end of my fertility quest. But I was having trouble accepting it. During this period, I sequestered myself. I hid from friends and family. I wasn't pleasant to be around. I was my own worst enemy, despising myself. I was acting like a bitch, as if to say, "See? I'm not worthy of friendship or love."

I met with my doctor to discuss next steps in family planning and told him how much I was grieving. He calmly said, "I have someone I'd like you to meet." And he set up a session with a grief counselor. Over the course of several months, she completely shifted the way I was looking at things. She explained that by continuing to alienate myself from those I cared about most, I was on a self-destructive course.

She gave me an example of a personal acquaintance of hers, Joan, whose husband had left her for another woman. All of Joan's friends felt sorry for her. But, ten years later, she was still mourning and seeking sympathy, and it had become tiring to many people who no longer had the energy to support her story. People avoided her, as if to say, "Get over it already, and get on with your life." The therapist looked me straight in the eye and asked me, "How far are you going to take this?"

I was making my infertility into "my story." For the sake of my loved ones, especially my husband and son, I had to get better. I realized that, yes, infertility was part of my life but it was not the cross I was going to die on. I wanted—needed—to keep living.

Adoption gave me new focus. Now I was so excited, so certain, so tired of waiting. But this wasn't the case with my husband. I remember one heated discussion when Gordon made it clear he was not on board. Looking back, I can see his position. I was very emotional (read *hormonal*—it was one month after my miscarriage, and I was a mess), and I was rushing things. That night, we had an intense talk in which he shared how he really felt: "We have a great family (Ethan, Mom, and Dad). Why do you need more? You are not thinking clearly. You are rushing things without thinking this through. SLOW DOWN." I would never have admitted it at the time, but his logic was spot on. He always brings me back to center.

Maybe I was more comfortable with adoption because I'd been introduced to it early. My father adopted in his second marriage, which gave me a newborn sister and brother when I was in college. So, by now, I had nineteen years of experiencing how normal and wonderful adoption can be.

Meanwhile, I continued to try to "sell" my husband on adopting. Throughout our family-building process, I had been the driver. Now that I saw adoption as the answer, I continued in this role: "Get with the program, Gordon! Why aren't you on board?"

One day, after yet another discussion in which I'd pushed my husband so hard to move forward with adoption, he blurted out, "Okay! But I am only doing this for you!"

I went to my therapist and asked, a bit sarcastically, how I was supposed to respond to that comment. She said, "You should say, 'Thank you!' He loves and trusts you so much that he is standing beside you." That was an eye-opening moment for me, as it was different from anything I'd considered. My initial reaction was to continue to push him, or blow up in anger, or cry in desperation. Instead, after coming home from my session, I showed Gordon my appreciation for his support and love.

I should have known this was the correct response. I've had extensive training in sales and marketing and understand when you get the answer you want, you say "thank you" and shut up. Do not sell past the close!

Thankfully, Gordon is the rational one, reeling me in when needed. But I really wanted this and he listened. I also realized we didn't need to be 100 percent in lockstep on the pacing, and we could still make it work. If you'll excuse the analogy, a couple will never be on the same level of "hungry"—I might be starving and want appetizers and an entrée and dessert; Gordon might want a long cocktail hour first, then the entrée. When I stopped selling *to* Gordon and, instead, spoke *with* Gordon about my strong wish, we did get in sync.

I knew adoption was right for us. And, when we fast-forward to the moment he first held our daughter, he and I were in complete agreement that it was the perfect decision for our family.

Chapter ♡ Two
A Road Less Traveled

How do you start down the path of adoption? Each woman took different baby steps. Yet their approaches had two big common themes. Number one: They educated themselves–fast. They put themselves on the most crash, intensive, accelerated course of study they'd ever undertaken. They devoured information, then went back for more. Number two: They talked to lots and lots of people. They shared. They listened. They supported and were supported. They were willing to get personal with strangers going through the same thing (though bonding came quickly).

Sydney

Our closest friends, Ginger and Gordon, started the adoption process a few months after we decided this was the road for us. I remember it like yesterday. Ginger poured herself into writing an "expecting mom" letter, so focused and determined to find a second child through adoption that the task didn't take them long. I never wanted to distract them from their outreach by asking how to start ours, so I sat back, watched, and waited. I had a few conversations with friends of friends, and I learned a lot about the process and system very rapidly—so much so, it was almost daunting.

It wasn't until the beautiful outcome of a baby girl came into Ginger and Gordon's lives that I realized: *If you believe it will happen, it will and can.* I was in such awe of their adoption experience that I imitated every step I could remember.

They had hired an adoption attorney considered to be the Cadillac of the industry. They'd also come up with some clever outreaches on their own, which led to connections with a few prospects. I was struck by how they didn't lose hope or focus until the day they got word that their expecting mom was pregnant with a baby girl.

Just months later, my husband and I met with Ginger and Gordon's adoption attorney. We rushed through every detail of the process so fast, we got introduced within a week to a young woman who was placing her three-year-old daughter. At that early point in our journey, based on our ages, we thought any child under three would be a joy in our lives. It wasn't until we met the three-year-old that we realized we really felt the need to parent for our first time with an infant. Meeting our first mom so quickly was the best thing that could have happened. It showed us our own determination, commitment, and partnership in this new world of adoption.

It was both fun and scary to meet a mom so fast. I left my first meeting with her wanting to help *her* just as much as I wanted to help her child. Knowing that the biological parent was placing her child in a better home than she could provide pulled my heartstrings like nothing ever has.

Dear ♡ Child

Elle

To begin the adoption process, I made an after-work appointment for Jack and me to join a Q&A session in our city on "How to Begin the Process" of adoption. I remember we were one of the first couples to walk into the room. I remember feeling completely nervous, wondering how we measured up to the others attending this thing. Did we look like we would cut it as adoptive parents? Did I look too un-mom-like in my tie-dye jeans, rocker T-shirt, and black blazer? I thought to myself, *Oh, hell, maybe I should've worn my black Theory suit that I use when I go to funerals or court (because I am serious about adoption, damn it!).* I told myself to calm down—at least I wore my black Theory blazer and Jack looked so Daddy Warbucks-like: casually cool and in control of the room in his dark denim jeans, blue-and-white-checked, button-down shirt (with the sleeves ALWAYS rolled up, because his "monkey" arms are so long that nothing off the rack fits him), and Converse sneakers.

As other prospective adoptive parents filed into the room, my nerves began to calm. We were instructed by the female moderator to put on stupid nametags and take a packet and sit down in the semicircle of chairs facing a green chalkboard. Next, we went around our semicircle and told everyone a bit about ourselves in typical "ice-breaker" fashion. We were asked to include a topic or question we'd like to discuss or get answered.

Two hours later, when the meeting came to a close, my mind was spinning out of control with so many questions and unknowns—so many what-ifs—that the whole adoption idea suddenly seemed terribly daunting. But, as we stepped out onto Post Street and headed for a glass of wine— or three—to take the edge off, Jack took my hand and said, "This is going to be easy." Those six little words settled my spinning—and made me fall even more deeply in love with this man.

We would get through this process. Not only would we get through it, we would come out the other end as better individuals and partners to each other and to our baby, who was somewhere out there in the universe waiting to meet us.

Over drinks and dinner after that first meeting, we decided that domestic adoption was the way to go for us. It was less costly, and we suspected it would happen much faster. Besides, we were getting used to the idea of an open adoption—that is the norm these days for domestic adoptions. Last, why go abroad when there are thousands of kids right here in the good ole' U.S. of A. who need loving homes?

Before that meeting, I was sure we'd go for an international adoption. But I'd been severely misled—the media is 100 percent to blame for this. I mean, look at Angelina Jolie and Madonna. They make it look so easy: you just get on a plane, fly to a country, and pick up a kid, right? Hey, they're getting a baby and saving a village at the same time! That's what star power will get you.

But sitting there at the meeting, I learned the realities of international adoption: Be prepared to make a few *long* visits to the country before you ultimately leave the place with baby in tow. These visits will be costly. And the process can take much longer than a domestic adoption. I also didn't like that, in almost all international adoptions, the baby would have spent nine months or more in an orphanage, stuck in a crib crying, with little or no human contact. One wonders how much this terrible start in life affects a child's well-being. I realized that I wanted to be there from birth, although we were still open to an older child.

After this first meeting, we also decided to use a small- to mid-sized adoption agency. And we found one: a local agency that felt right to us. Making those two key decisions—domestic adoption and choosing our adoption agency—really helped jump-start everything. I made the call and signed us up for our first "getting to know the agency" meeting. We were finally getting somewhere!

A week later, we joined about twenty-five people in a room at the agency—singles and couples, gay and straight, all in search of their baby. There we were, sitting there, measuring each other up. We were full of questions, anxiety, and hope. Bella, that night's speaker, walked us through her adoption story: the agency, the timelines, what to expect, what monies were expected to be dropped in the process, and general FAQs. Next, three couples who were newly with child, told us about their adoption journeys. The journeys were all very different yet, at the same time, exactly the same. (Sort of like us four women in this book—each, in her own way, full of life, love, strength, and openness to take on the unknown.)

We left this meeting full of excitement and hope. Before it ended, Bella told everyone, "All of you will find your baby. Period." As much as I wanted to believe her, I wasn't 100 percent convinced. But, guess what? She was so right. Ironically, we found our baby nine months later. And what's even cooler is that eleven months after that afternoon, Bella asked my baby girl, Harper, and me to be guest speakers for newcomers to the agency.

Ginger

One thing that helped Gordon and me start the process was educating ourselves about what the future would likely hold for us. We'd already teamed up on a home remodel, and I saw this in the same way: start with the end in mind. How do we get from Point A to Point B? Here was our plan (it worked):

First, we connected with experts. I'd heard about an attorney in San Francisco who was well connected. Why reinvent the wheel, right?

Second, we learned as much as we could about something we knew very little about. Instead of visiting the Home Depot every weekend, we sent an email to everyone we knew, asking if they knew someone who had adopted. If yes, we requested that they connect with us, so we could learn from their experience. We got back a huge flow of info.

It is true what they say: knowledge is power. Good adoption experience or bad, we learned something from each conversation with those who had traveled the path before us. This knowledge helped us feel more confident in our decision to adopt.

We also became very open about our interest in adoption. This was going a little against the grain, as we are relatively private people. But I found that the more I *talked* about considering adoption, the more comfortable it felt.

Julia

The task of knowing where to start was daunting, to say the least. Even though my friend Sydney had just completed the process, we were in a different state with different laws. She could only help me with advice about *her* process which, as I was soon to find out, was different from what mine was going to be.

I knew I wanted to use Sydney's facilitator, Hope, who worked with birth moms in California. But it was so confusing trying to figure out how to adopt a baby from California while we were in Colorado! I felt like I was trying to make my way through a dim hallway where I could see the light way at one end, but kept falling over furniture that was hidden in the darkness in front of me. The obstacles seemed endless.

I needed to figure out which laws governed adoption in the two states, understand their different requirements, and fully understand what was illegal. I called several agencies and attorneys in both Colorado and California, only to receive conflicting information and end up more confused. For instance, Colorado law prohibits the use of adoption facilitators like Hope. For several days after speaking with one attorney, I was under the impression that we couldn't use Hope at all to find a birth mom. But then, after consulting with another attorney, we learned there were ways Colorado law would allow it. Conflicting information like this was around every corner. Surely, we were not the first people to ever adopt a California baby in Colorado. So why couldn't anyone set the record straight for me?

To make matters more difficult, my husband was over the age limit for several of our local adoption agencies. Even though Oscar was healthier and more youthful than most men half his age, many agencies had a rigid age cap of fifty-five years. Oddly, several of these same agencies would allow a single woman of my age to adopt. Apparently having no husband at all was preferable to having one who was "too old."

All I wanted was a child of my own, one Oscar and I could raise together and love. I didn't understand why the adoption process was *so* difficult, *so* confusing and *so* expensive! It was like adding insult to injury: not only could I not get pregnant, but the laws made adopting a child incredibly complicated.

After filtering through the local agencies, phone call after phone call, we finally found one that fit us. During my first phone call with their administrator, wary from previous rejections, I asked what their age limit was. The woman almost laughed, and even sounded confused. She replied that their policy was to review each family, case by case, and determine their individual potential as parents, rather than making a rule that excluded deserving families who didn't fit the "norm." Their openness gave me hope.

We applied and were accepted, and we began the home study process.

As they waded in more deeply, sometimes things seemed to be go-

ing fast—too fast. Other times, things seemed to drag on and on.

Privately, each woman couldn't help but add this time to the time

they had already spent on other paths. Emotionally, they were

performing a high-wire balancing act: be open and ready to take

an enormous plunge at the drop of a hat... but keep hope realistic

and, under control, so it doesn't unhinge you.

Julia

Overall, our adoption process was fast, but that's not to say it didn't have its ups and downs. We knew from Sydney that her facilitator, Hope, worked with a lot of expecting moms and had a great track record of open adoptions. Yet we were completely shocked when she placed us with a birth mom before we were even completely in her program! I'd only emailed her a draft of my expecting mom letter in the hope that a new girl she was working with would consider us.

When Hope told us the news through email, we were excited and scared at the same time. We had a ton of questions to ask, but we were out of the country on vacation at the time. We thought we could wait to respond until we returned. But when we returned home, we found out that the birth mom had gone with her second choice family. I was devastated. I didn't know how devastated I was until, months later, we still hadn't gotten another potential match. Was that going to be our only chance, and did we blow it?

Hope told us from the beginning that Oscar's age would be a challenge. Would another birth mom ever choose us? I tried not to focus on it. I tried to be okay with the idea that we might never get chosen. In a way, I felt like that lonely grade-school kid on the playground, hoping to be chosen for a game of kickball.

We passed the year mark from when we'd started the whole process. Oscar began tossing around the idea of trying IVF again. I didn't want to go down that road again, but I was starting to doubt we'd ever be chosen. Reluctantly, I made an appointment with the fertility doctor. Our consultation was two months out. I remember hanging up the phone and praying to God that if He wanted us to adopt, He had two months to make something happen. PLEASE!! Make something happen.

Ginger

Once we got going, we attended several seminars at our adoption attorney's office and also at our adoption agency. None of these were one on one; rather, they were more like support groups. The sessions had different themes, like interracial adoption and how to introduce adoption to members of your family.

The counselors leading these groups were great. But the most valuable part for me was being with other people in the same situation. We met people of every demographic, yet everyone had a common bond. It really helped to share stories and experiences as the adoption process unfolded. Also helpful was chatting with my husband afterward to compare notes—what was interesting to him, were there any aha moments, did it help talking to husbands who are also dealing with anxious wives hungry to raise a family?

There is one memorable comment from a counselor: when you are a prospective adoptive parent, you are asked to completely commit (i.e., drop everything if a lead comes in) and, at the same time, *not* be committed to the point where you have false expectations and make yourself crazy. It is a tough balance. Just hearing her say that helped me a lot.

Sydney

Knowing what I know now, I feel that much of the pace of an adoption is controlled by the adopting parents—how well you navigate the system, how fast you complete the home study process, how aggressive you are with your outreach, and whether you use a facilitator.

Once we were placed, I saw that using a facilitator—as our birth mom did—is the most direct line to a match. A state-licensed adoption agency can take the longest, though that wasn't the case for Elle and Jack. I also learned that while your adoption attorney hooks up with your adoption agency at a certain point, and can also lead you to a facilitator in the early stages—which ours did, and OMG, she was a gem!—the attorney doesn't really contribute to your outreach. That said, there are many productive paths to the outcome you want: a baby.

The process seemed to take so long getting started, especially since I was already three years into trying to build a family. I felt discouraged about ever fulfilling that dream, based on my later-in-life start, my own reproductive issues, and the many hopeful but unsuccessful attempts with a surrogate, followed by weeks, months, and years of struggling to accept that being without a family might be okay.

Support groups seemed empty. One of my funniest memories of those sessions still leaves me laughing today. It is a story I'll share with my son when he can understand adoption. I went to a group meeting at our attorney's office, and sat around with mixed- and same-gender adopting families. We did some of the craziest activities to prepare for meeting with the birth mom for the first time and to understand the emotions of everyone involved. My husband was out of town, so I had to participate with a stand-in husband, which made the exercise seem even less real. It didn't help that we used dolls wrapped in scarves to practice passing off the adoptive baby to one another! Looking back, I can smile, seeing it was part of the process and part of accepting what you go through. That truth wasn't obvious along the way, but is very clear *now*!

Chapter ♡ Three
Dear Birth Mom

Julia, Elle, Sydney, and Ginger all have marketing and sales ex-
perience. Their husbands are bright, talented men. Yet none of it
prepared any of them for creating the expecting mom letter. It had
to be genuine, yet it had to sell you. You and your husband had
to look happy, but not OVERLY *content with your present life. The*
staged photos had to look spontaneous! It was all consuming. No
work project had ever meant so much. They got tons of advice.
Then the advice-givers sat back, smiled, and said, "Of course, it
has to sound like you."

Sydney

I quickly learned that writing the expecting mom letter was the most important part of the process. I was determined not to let it take too long and to make the letter fun and engaging. Our friends and our adoption attorney gave me a lot of advice about what was important to include. They all repeated that, above all else, it needs to feel like us.

Meeting a birth mom before we were ready had opened my eyes. I knew we had to provide her with reassurances of security, love, and openness in order to gain her trust.

Writing the expecting mom letter is like a test of your readiness to adopt. Until you can sit down and put to paper what you feel, who you are, what you have gone through to start a family, and how it brought you to the world of adoption, you are not ready. Once you get this very emotional process started and completed, the rest is up to the universe and the goodness of the adoption world. Everything else, like home study, background check, and creative outreach is just a *process*. In fact, it was the process itself that sometimes demotivated me. Our adoption attorney operated by the book, and our adoption agency seemed bureaucratic. The wonder, miracle, and fulfillment of a child being placed into our home often felt far away.

They say most birth moms don't read the letters from the adopting parents. Instead, they look at your photos as they think, *This is the life I will chose for my child* and *This is the life I wish I could give my child.* We learned quickly that photos with kids were a must, photos of our family and lifestyle were also important— no sunglasses. At one point, our adoption attorney staff told us we had too many photos with water in them! I was beside myself trying to figure out the picture part. But once it started coming together, I realized our life together had been well captured in our 8"x10" brochure and that it was beautiful. Although, of course, we were similar to everyone else seeking to adopt a child, we felt we were in a world of our own… one filled with some apprehension and much joyous anticipation.

Elle

Writing the expecting mom letter was a huge deal. It took me (not Jack—he was fine with the first draft—I'm the detail-oriented perfectionist) *six months* to write. I kept writing and then rewriting it. Jack and I started working on it while we were in Tokyo on a business trip and also celebrating our tenth wedding anniversary. We began writing it together over a glass—or three—of wine (to pluck up our courage and confidence) on a bullet train from Tokyo to Kyoto. Kyoto was going to be the fun anniversary part after Jack's work in Tokyo.

I was completely frozen. I mean, what does one say? How do you make yours stand out from every other expecting mother letter? Counselors at our agency gave us samples of other letters, and the one that stood out for me was written by a male gay couple who would have used a *trash* magazine layout. I loved this approach because it targeted the audience who was going to be reading the letters: young girls who buy those crappy mags. I loved how the layout stood out from all the other blah blah blah, "We are a great couple; pick us" letters.

After putting our own *US Weekly*-type mag layout together and presenting it to our counselor at the agency, Shelley, we got lousy news. We had to give her all new pictures of us because in all our shots, we were sporting sunglasses, baseball caps (Jack's bald—I mean, he shaves his head. I'm not allowed to say the b-word. But what do you expect? He has to wear caps.), and wine glasses. She asked us to use pictures of us hanging with kids. Hell, we don't really hang with kids. So, the next thing you know, we're hiking with friends and their kids or volunteering to go to the zoo!

Julia

When it was time to put together our expecting mom letter, my OCD—I prefer to call it my "perfectionism"—came out. Often, when I want to do something just right, I become paralyzed before I even begin. I struggled for a long time before beginning to write. Putting it down in print felt so final. I definitely didn't want to make any mistakes.

The task felt like it would take forever to get absolutely perfect and complete. The graphic layout came pretty easily. As an architect with an eye for design, I knew how I wanted the letter to appear: clean lines with a bit of whimsy. I decided on a sophisticated navy for the main color (is that why we ended up with a boy?), with a border of gray and green swirls as an accent. It represented not only my design philosophy, but also my outlook on life. A serious but never too serious perspective.

The photos were another story. I am not a "picture" person, being terribly un-photogenic. What's more, Oscar and I didn't typically take family pictures. So we had to stage many photos. We didn't want them to look fake, but I also knew we had to portray our entire lives on two pages, so they had to say a lot. These pages had to say we were fun and active, that we loved being outdoors and with family. And we loved children! So we took photos of me with my niece and nephews, and Oscar with his granddaughters.

Once we'd portrayed ourselves in pictures, I moved on to the text. That was the biggest challenge. In a way, it was amusing to sort out the facts of our lives into what was important and what could be left on the cutting room floor. It was also more than a little disappointing to edit out things that are important to… our spiri-tuality, for example… because it might put off potential biological mamas.

Oscar was my editor and proofreader. And Sydney was a tremendous help since she'd already been through it. Having her experienced eye review the letter gave me confidence. When she and Hope gave it a good review we were done. I had the final product printed at a local print shop and mailed the letters off to our agency along with a prayer.

Ginger

For me, writing the expecting mom letter was the worst part of the adoption expe-rience. I was already very fragile and raw. I put intense pressure on myself and my family to get a "perfect" letter together. A big part of this was pictures. Anywhere we went, I was ready with my camera, remembering our adoption attorney's instructions: no hats or sunglasses, no bathing suits, and make sure there is "room" in your photo for another member of the family. I tortured my family with several photo shoots.

Since I have some marketing experience, you'd think I could put together a simple brochure. But this was far too personal and far too important. Fun? No. Although, at one point, I did manage a chuckle when I realized I'd *spent over two hours looking for the ideal shade of green for our brochure.* Looking back, I see how ridiculous it was: a birth mother is going to pick us because she likes the colors in our brochure? No. But at the time, I was so obsessively focused on the letter, I was over-thinking the whole thing. It was like I was trying on endless outfits and asking everyone frantically if my butt looked big.

I asked friends, relatives, and anyone who had any design or branding experience (poor Sydney was called upon!) for their input. If it was not just right, I thought we might miss an opportunity. Truth be told, I even did some Photoshop work on the picture of our home to make the grass look greener. Nuts.

And there is so much coaching from the adoption professionals, like, "Don't have Ethan (our son) on the front cover photo because a birth mother might eliminate you as a candidate if she regards your family as already complete and happy." Huh? He is a part of our family, why hide him?

A good piece of advice we received was that there will be *one* thing that a biological mother likes about you and your family, and that *one* thing will swing everything in your favor. A friend of a friend was favored because there were musical interests in the home. My advice is don't try to find that one thing; just be yourself. Our eventual birth mom, Amber, liked us because we had an older sibling for her baby, so there!

Chapter ♡ Four
Match Made in Heaven

There was no getting around it. They had to go through it. Each woman had to keep her heart open as she sought the birth mom whose sweet yes would give her a happiness beyond anything she'd known. First came the false leads, each one a small heartbreak a biological mother she would never know, a child she would never hug. Throughout, each woman had to stay open and let herself be wounded. She had to accept missed phone calls and no-show, surprise reversals and vanishing acts. Sometimes searching for the birth mom felt exciting, like dating. Sometimes it felt like hell. But it was the one path to the heaven of a baby.

Elle

While we were getting our materials together at the adoption agency, I had two false leads on a baby. The first came from a regular client at my boutique. She was an attorney named Tara, a single woman who had gone through the adoption process and won at it… adopting her beautiful daughter, Mackenzie. Tara walked me through her experience and gave me names of adoption attorneys and facilitators. Besides giving me a wealth of knowledge, she gave me hope and inspired me.

A few months after our "adoption powwow," I got an email from Tara, explaining that the biological mother of Mackenzie, Patti, was pregnant again; she asked if I would be interested. Well you damn well know I was interested. I was WAY past just interested. I remember trembling with joy as I read her email about how Patti was looking for a family to adopt her unborn baby.

I immediately called Tara and she repeated what I'd just read. The next thing I know, I was in my car dialing Patti's cell number and leaving a voice mail. I explained my link to Tara and introduced myself. A few days later, we set up a phone meeting. But that phone meeting never happened. I was back to square one. I felt so discouraged because a big-ass carrot was dangled, and I never even got to show the biological mother who I was.

I know Tara felt horrible, and I think she felt partly to blame for this wild goose chase (which is ridiculous), because a few months later, almost to make it up to me, she called me again about a lead in Kazakhstan (yes, the hometown of Borat). A friend of Tara's father, who did business in Kazakhstan, had a girlfriend there. This girlfriend's young sister had gotten knocked up. The girl couldn't even support herself, much less a baby. Tara's father's friend was supporting the pregnant young girl, but at her request, he was trying to find an adoptive family for the unborn baby.

My husband Jack and I had a dozen calls with this very gracious and kind man who was helping the pregnant woman. What we learned was it would take months upon months to get this baby legally. Even if we were to go over there, it would be ages before we would come home with the baby. Eventually, we lost contact with this gentleman. I still wonder whatever happened to the young girl and the baby I was trying so hard to make ours.

Sydney

For a while, I was so wrapped up in comparing our expecting mom letter to the letters of other families, I felt overwhelmed and as if I had zero control over what was happening. Then there were the emotional swings. After we passed our home study, our agency began pursuing various birth mom leads. That meant we'd receive a call or email letting us know about a birth mom, and asking if we'd agree to be presented to her. Of course, our hopes immediately zoomed sky high. But the alert only meant that the birth mom would receive our letter. There was no guarantee of anything. I had so many highs and lows, the excitement of knowing our letter was in the hands of a half-dozen birth moms during any given month. There was a crash to reality, knowing the moms were reviewing our letter *along with the letters of many other prospect families.*

Soon we started actually meeting birth moms. Each meeting involved huge pressure. But there was a fun "dress-up" side to the meetings, as Phillip and I worked so hard on presenting ourselves in the right manner. Yes, he and I would literally change our clothes five times before deciding we looked okay. One time, we came out of our closets dressed like twins!

Driving to meet the moms, we'd go back and forth about what we were going to ask them and what we wanted to share. We were keyed up and excited. The experience felt almost like going on a first date… with the odd twist that we were going *together* to meet our date!

But my reality was far from all laughter at our matching outfits. For months, every birth mom lead turned out to be a dead end. I felt discouraged. *Would this path, too, come to nothing?* I thought. Then, on one afternoon…

The day we got "the Call," it was like God was speaking over a loudspeaker in my living room. I was all alone because my husband was in Germany on a business trip. I danced with joy until late at night. It was our third biological mother connection but the first mom I would meet alone.

The phone call was from Hope, the biological mother's facilitator. And right away, things felt different. Hope reassured me that this connection would turn into a match. It was the first time anyone had gone into full detail about the biological mother and about where Phillip and I stood with respect to other potential adoptive families being considered. She told me that the mom, Quinn, was choosing among three families (my heart sank) but that both she and the biological dad's mother liked Phillip and me best (my spirits soared). And it was the first time anyone had actually strategized my meeting with the birth mom to give us the greatest advantage. Hope thought it was important that we be second in line to meet with her, so she had one family before and after to compare us to. Then she asked me, "Do you want a boy or girl?" When I replied that it didn't matter, she said, "Girlfriend, you are having a boy!" I couldn't feel anything but matched! Hope truly gave me hope.

In the following weeks and months, Phillip and I learned that Hope had the biggest heart on the planet. Navigating the system through her finally felt real and right. She will always be a part of our family, and she is the first person to whom I refer others when I they are thinking about adoption. Hope made the entire process such a celebration. And she made the outcome so secure and joyful.

Elle

On April 20, 2010, at eleven a.m., I got "the Call." I had just arrived at work and was in a horrible mood. I was in the process of closing my stores, which I'd had for almost a decade, and I was trying to put on a happy face for my employees, who were now about to be without jobs, and for my customers, because I was trying to keep the store closing a secret in order to get full retail dollars off what was left on my racks. I was standing behind the cash wrap, going over the day's to-dos with Ashley, my store manager, when my cell phone rang. An unknown number flashed up. Usually I don't answer unknown numbers. But, for some reason, that morning I decided to. Here's how the call went:

Me: Hello?

Megan: Hi, Elle?

Me: Yes, this is she.

Megan: Hi, Elle. This is Megan from the adoption agency. Are you sit-

ting down?

Me: No. Is everything okay?

Megan: You might want to sit down… are you sitting yet?

Me: Yes. What's up?

Megan: You, my dear, have been selected by a birth mother! The baby is going to be born in twenty-three days!

[Reader, did I mention yet that twenty-three is my lucky number?]

Me: OMG!!!! (This is when my chest popped in my mouth, and I just sat there feeling like I was in a Charlie Brown episode… blah blah blah blah blah blah blah blah… Megan was talking and my mind was racing. I could hear her talking to me, but I couldn't catch anything she was saying because I was beyond excitement.)

Over the next few minutes, Megan told me that the biological mother, Rachel, was eight months' pregnant and that she'd had no medical care up to that point. Nola, Rachel's godmother, was the mediator for her and her mom, and they all decided that adoption was the answer. Our agency had sent a packet of hundreds of expecting mother letters for Rachel to review, and she picked… us. We were her only pick. Later, Megan faxed me a ten-page form of general questions the agency had asked Rachel and Dan, the biological father. I read—no, I devoured—the questions and their answers.

Now Megan told me Rachel wanted to talk via phone the very next day. I was giddy with excitement; I could hardly contain myself. Megan arranged for me to call Rachel.

For the next twenty-four hours, I was over the moon. The biggest weight/dark cloud had been lifted off me. I was undeniably the happiest person alive. Period. I decided to drive an hour north to tell Jack in person that we'd just found our baby and she'd be here in twenty-three days. My lucky number twenty-three again! He was at a week-long off-site work meeting.

Jack walked into the hotel room during an afternoon break from his meetings. I had the biggest smile on my face. I told him the incredible news and showed him

Megan's faxed questionnaire, which made it seem so real. It was really happening! Jack was cautious but excited. We had dinner that night with Jack's team, and spouses were invited. Jack and I mingled with the crowd that night, but didn't share "our secret" with anyone. Throughout the evening, we found one another, exchanged special smiles, and winked knowingly. We were "expecting," FINALLY!

Julia

A year into the process, with nothing to show for it, I promised Oscar I'd meet with a fertility doctor to discuss trying IVF again. But my heart wasn't in it. I waited and procrastinated in filling out my medical questionnaire. Someone with history of endometriosis, infertility, stroke, and adrenal failure does not have a short history. I always dread the paperwork.

About a month before our appointment, I finally sat down to fill out the stack of forms. First page: name, address, date of birth, etc.... Second page: my phone beeped... it was a text from Hope! *She had a birth mom who was interested in us!*

I don't believe in coincidences. I think it was divine timing. I balled up the medical questionnaire and threw it in the trash.

Quickly, Hope explained she was at lunch with a girl who "loved" our profile. She said she'd call after her meeting. So I sat and stared at my phone. Nothing. An hour went by and I was pacing. How long does lunch take? Was she looking at other people's profiles? Maybe she'd find someone she liked better. Maybe once she learned more about us she would change her mind.

The time passed excruciatingly slowly. I was trying to busy myself with tidying up the house when my phone finally rang. We were at the top of this birth mom's list! Hope said she *especially loved Oscar!* We'd always feared his age would be one of our biggest obstacles in being chosen, but this girl, Laura, loved the fact that he had raised three sons and was an experienced father. And now we might have the chance to be the parents of a boy!

I was elated! I was jumping up and down, but then Hope told me something else. We had more waiting to do. Laura wanted to take our profile home to discuss the choice with her boyfriend. The fact that she was taking this decision so seriously both encouraged and frightened me. Obviously, she cared a great deal about the baby she was carrying. But were we enough? Were we "it"?

In the adoption process, the waiting period is never over. It just shifts from one aspect to another. So now we were waiting again. This time, for the final decision from the biological dad. Hope said she'd call us in the morning. Neither of us slept much that night.

The phone rang just before noon. It was a chilly Saturday in February and Oscar and I were painting. A few weeks earlier, I decided it would be a good idea to freshen up our living room. We were rolling a sophisticated grey onto our walls when the phone rang. I put it on speaker phone and said hello. "Are you ready to be a momma??!!" Hope's voice on the other end of the line made me feel like I'd just won the lottery!

I was in shock for quite some time. Not only was the reality that we had been chosen not sinking in, but the fact that the baby was due in about a month was hard to believe.

The day we learned we'd been chosen, I called my parents and my sister. We all cried—I think my sister the most! She had wanted this for me as much as and for as long as I had. My family was so excited for us, and I knew I was safe in sharing with them. When I got off the phone with my family, my mind was numb… and racing at the same time! Was this actually happening? Would we be ready?

I had so much to do to prepare. But there was always that tiny nagging feeling that something would go wrong. Laura would change her mind. There would be a problem with the pregnancy. Oscar would change his mind. Any number of ideas—realistic or crazy—ran through my head. For this reason, I only shared our good news with close friends and family. The prospect of explaining why I didn't have a baby—*again*—was too painful. After I miscarried, the questions of friends or acquaintances who hadn't heard the bad news brought grief over and over. I couldn't deal with that again.

Cautiously, I began to make preparations. I painted the nursery, purchased furniture (but kept the receipts!), and began to think of names. A close friend and my sister wanted to throw me a baby shower. I insisted that we only do one AFTER the baby was home with us. There were too many variables to commit to a shower before his arrival.

I was excited—how could I not be? I was going to be a mom, I hoped!

Ginger

Over the course of our outreach, we had a couple of leads. I was trying to practice what I'd learned from an adoption counselor, who said that a biological mother is looking to place because she is *not* in an ideal situation to raise a child. This was a delicate way of saying, if you are looking for a perfectly healthy young woman who has been eating organic veggies between regularly scheduled doctor visits for the last nine months, you have a false set of expectations.

I'll admit that at first it was a struggle not to apply my standards to these young birth moms. But, over time, I came to see and to deeply feel that this was not a time to judge behavior or question character. I couldn't use my moral standards to evaluate a birth mom's decisions. I hadn't lived in her world. I wasn't raised in the same environment by the same role models or lack thereof. My upbringing took place in a two-parent, middle-class home where I was loved, encouraged, praised. How could I evaluate a person who was not given the same opportunities?

One day, our adoption attorney, Melinda, called us about a birth mom in Ohio. Amber was a woman in her mid-twenties who had placed previously, and was interested in speaking with us. My attempt to connect was unsuccessful. She answered the phone while she was shopping and promised to call me back... but never did. I figured that was that. I felt sorry this opportunity fell through, as Melinda had spoken very positively about Amber's interest in working with us. But actually, it was easy to move on; I hadn't invested much emotional energy in the situation at that point.

A birth mother has expressed strong interest in you, and you are giddy with happiness. And a nervous wreck. Will she choose you? For keeps? You are so terribly eager to hear her voice, to sense who she is. Julia and Sydney, and their husbands, met with the young woman who expressed interest in placing with them. Elle spoke with the birth mom on the phone. (For Ginger, events moved too fast to offer the chance.) So what do you say to this person on the phone? What do you wear when you meet the woman who is possibly carrying your child? How on earth do you act naturally?

Elle

That night in the hotel room, I couldn't sleep. I was so nervous about the phone call the next day with Rachel, scheduled for noon. What should I say? How should I act? I had that nervous feeling you get before an interview. But the nervous feeling was even more intense because of what was at stake: our baby. I didn't want to screw anything up…

The next morning, I jotted down a few questions for Rachel. My head was spinning so fast, I even wrote out how I'd introduce myself to her. I didn't want these first words to come out as the "whirling dervish" in my head.

For my first words to Rachel, I wrote: "I'm so honored you have chosen me to talk with today… I know that you must be dealing with so much right now. Anything that you want to ask about me, bring it up! I don't know about you, Rachel, but I am nervous as hell right now." Later, on the phone, that last statement really broke the ice between us. I acknowledged that we were both nervous and scared and I let her know I was going to be an open book to her.

I called Rachel at noon on the dot. She didn't answer. I proceeded to panic and let every worst-case scenario play out in my head. OMG, she'd backed out… she didn't want to go through with the adoption… she found another family… maybe her or Dan's parents decided to take on the baby. It just wasn't fair—*she hadn't even met me yet.*

I sat there frozen, staring at the piece of paper with my notes written on it, and began to feel tears coming down my cheeks and falling onto the paper, making the black-inked words run. I was devastated. Sixteen minutes later, I decided to text Rachel, thinking this could be a better way to make contact. For the next three hours and five minutes, I was a complete wreck… then the most amazing thing happened: a text popped up from Rachel. Our first official contact was made.

Rachel's text read, "Hi, Elle. This is Rachel. I'm very sorry I missed you, but I am at work until five p.m. your time. If you are free then, I would love to speak to you."

Whew! I began to breathe again… and texted her that I'd call her at eight p.m. her time, five p.m. my time. The next two hours trickled by. At five I called her, and got that feeling you get when you're on a first date with the hottest, most popular boy in school. I was so nervous and so giddy. All the same, our getting-to-know-each-other call went well.

At the end of the call, Rachel asked me to call a "family friend" in the San Francisco Bay Area. This turned out to be Nola, her godmother. I called Nola the next day and we instantly hit it off. We set up a beautiful poolside lunch for the next day, at a hotel overlooking Napa Valley. Later, saying farewell to Nola, she confessed something: Rachel wanted her to screen us to make sure we were as great as we seemed. "I'll be proud to report back to her and her mom and dad that, yes, you guys are."

Sydney

After a number of meetings with various birth moms that led nowhere, we finally made a deep connection. We were one of three families the birth mom planned to see. Phillip was away on business, so she and I arranged a lunch date. The day of our meeting, I was so nervous. On the drive to the restaurant, I must have looked in the rearview mirror a hundred times. I wondered what the birth mom would think of me. I wanted her to have a sense of my style, but didn't want her to think I was *too* stylish to be a mom. I wanted to wow her with my cosmetics experience, so I brought her a bag of beauty goodies. I learned later she doesn't wear makeup! (However, her mom loved the brand I'd brought her.) Not for a second did I wonder what she looked like. The truth was, I didn't care. I was just grateful to meet a healthy mom who was willing to place her child in our life.

Once we were finally face to face, I was pleasantly surprised by how similar her coloring was to mine. Then came a second coincidence: Quinn described the bio-dad's coloring as being nearly identical to Phillip's. Looking back, I can't help but feel we were chosen because of Phillip's and the bio-dad's physical similarity. Knowing now that most birth moms make their choice based on photos, it's clear there was an instant attraction.

I was amazed by how comfortable the birth mom was at lunch. She told a few jokes, and was completely in control when it came to asking me questions. She'd brought her parents with her—the couple who had adopted her at age seven from a foster home. All three spoke openly about the bio-dad, explaining that his family supported her decision to place the baby for adoption, and revealing that we were his mother's choice among the three families. It was comforting to know there was acceptance on the bio-dad's side. It eased the worry about getting the signed consent from him, a legality that can linger throughout the process and sabotage the agreement at the last minute.

Our lunch lasted a good couple of hours, and the conversation flowed easily. Then came the three questions she'd prepared to ask us. Her first question was one I was so happy to answer with a definitive "yes": "Will you be a stay-at-home mom?" However, her second question wasn't nearly as easy to answer: "How much contact are you open to?" Later, Phillip and I decided we needed time to consider our response. Her third question was what sealed the placement, in my mind: "Can I name my son before I place him?" I answered, "Of course. What do you want to name him?" It was mind-blowing that her chosen name—Cole—was one of two names Phillip and I had chosen.

My meeting with the birth mom was left open-ended. A decision was dependent on us meeting again with my husband. Although there were still two other families in the picture, I secretly felt she favored us because she wanted the follow-up meeting with Phillip *and* there was the uncanny name connection.

That second meeting took place after Phillip had traveled fifteen hours straight, changed his clothes, and piled into our car for a two-hour drive to a Starbucks. I prepped him all the way there, and continued to talk about "our" son on a first-name basis. At one point, my husband said to me, "Do I have any say in this being the right birth mom?" Until that moment, it never dawned on me that we, too, could accept or reject, and I immediately began to fear yet another dead end. I now had to get Phillip's approval, along with the birth mom's. It was a very hot summer night. But I was sweating from more than the heat!

Luck was on our side this time. As soon as we arrived, I could tell Phillip felt comfortable and at ease with Quinn. Could this be it?

During our three-hour gathering with Quinn, her parents, and the facilitator, we all shared stories. Quinn got excited talking about being in her high school band and her love for the trumpet. She confessed that one of the things that had drawn her to us was reading in our expecting mom letter that Phillip played the cello when he was in high school. I had a good silent chuckle when she said that, since I'd complained at the time that all the advice we got to put those kinds of things in about ourselves seemed so crazy. I now see that you never know what someone will like about you.

Quinn had even brought a photo album to give us glimpses of her childhood and years growing up with her adopted family. It all felt so normal that Phillip and I both felt if this is our birth mom, we'll have a happy and healthy relationship through open adoption.

Yet we made no assumptions that we were her final choice for parents. In fact, we asked about other families she had met. The only time things seemed tense was when our contact agreement came up.

The contact agreement between the birth mom and us would pin down how much contact we'd have *and* what kind of relationship we'd have during the periods we weren't meeting in person. Just talking about it, as we now started to do over dessert and coffee, reminded us all that we'd be separating after the birth and then agreeing to come together during the year.

Before meeting that day, Phillip and I had given the question of future contact much thought. We'd decided a once-a-year visit would be enough, but sending photos and updates on how Cole was doing would be ongoing. It turned out Quinn wanted to meet with Cole twice a year, which seemed too much like co-parenting to us.

As the contact agreement now became the focus of our discussion, everything that was starting to feel like ours suddenly felt so far away. And that was when the first drama with Quinn happened. At the words "contact agreement," she left the table crying. Her mother and the facilitator rushed after her. Her father, Phillip, and I sat making small talk with uncertainty in our eyes.

It felt like an hour before Quinn returned to the table, but when she did, it was a moment that will be with us forever. She stood by our table and, in her confident and commanding way, said "Phillip, Sydney, will you please come outside?" We did, and as we stood before her, I could feel a sense of loss already building inside me. I felt my husband's hands of strength and encouragement holding mine. And I remember like nothing else in my life what she said to us: "I met with two other families." Phillip squeezed my hand, my mind washed with emotion and tears streamed down my cheeks. "And, yes, you should be hugging 'cause I want you to be the parents of my son."

All of us tearfully embracing, we returned inside and sat back down with a new sense of ease. The final choice had been made. We then returned to the delicate issue of the contact agreement. I thought quickly and suggested creating a Facebook page that Cole and Quinn could share. That made her so happy! I said I would start it instantly and, as it turned out, before Phillip and I even got home, she and her mom had both "friend-requested" me. The issue of contact was extremely sensitive, since I didn't really want them in my life, yet I was hoping for a way for Quinn to have a glimpse into Cole's life. The Facebook solution worked for everybody.

From the moment we were chosen as parents of this unborn child, we had three weeks to get to know Quinn. I was lucky she let me come along on her doctor appointments, and was relieved to find out how healthy her pregnancy had been. During that period, I learned more about Quinn personally. For the most part, she grew comfortable with us. It was a joyous three weeks. She told us she wanted us to be in the delivery room when she gave birth, and that she wanted us to be the first to hold the baby, and hoped that Phillip would stay up by her head, so she wouldn't be exposed, but also said he could cut the cord.

Over and over, Quinn let us know she was very happy about choosing us. As the weeks flew by, we all—members of both families—shared a lot. Quinn posted Facebook updates with positive thoughts she wanted to share with Cole. Her mom posted songs to Cole about what the wonderful life he was being born into. I posted pictures of things I was buying to prepare for Cole being in our life. I continued to send Quinn gifts that I put a lot of thought into, and to plan fun things to do after our weekly doctor visits.

During one lunch date with Phillip and me, Quinn shared a story about how she was devastated and heartbroken that the bio-dad hadn't stayed in a relationship with her. She told us a lot about their eight months together. Quinn also described how she thought she was having early labor at seven months, and packed up a bag for the hospital. As she was telling us the story, she turned and looked at me, saying, "You're going to want to make sure you pack a bag for Phillip, too. You know the stuff he'll need to keep busy while waiting for the baby to be born." She was amazingly adult at the young age of nineteen, and very respectful of our future with her son and the open adoption we were about to share.

Julia

After the preliminary match with Laura, we decided to schedule a lunch to meet her and the biological dad. Oscar and I flew to California for a long weekend. His parents live in the area, so it became a family reunion as well.

But the morning after we got there, I got a call from Hope, our facilitator, telling us Laura was in the hospital with contractions. We knew she was ready to have the baby and move on with her life, but this was way too early. My heart was in my throat as Oscar and I prayed all afternoon that her labor would stop and she'd go home. And she did! We were relieved that we wouldn't be meeting Benjamin (as we had already named him) on this trip. He needed to wait at least three more weeks. But then we weren't certain if Laura would be up for our lunch the following Monday. Was the trip in vain? Luckily, she recovered over the weekend and we were on!

Meeting a biological parent is like going on a blind date. What will they look like? Will we get along? Will we have anything in common? There are the same unknowns, fears, and uncertainties—except for the fact that this was much more important! We'd never spoken, emailed, or texted. And, because of our geographical distance, this was our one and only chance to make a good impression.

The morning of our meeting, I had sweaty palms, a sick stomach, and my mind was racing. What would I wear? Dress up and bling out or play it safe and tone it down? After about five wardrobe changes, I finally decided on a simple long-sleeve shirt and skinny jeans. I was comfortable, and I decided that was important. Oscar, always classy, wore a dress shirt, jeans, and loafers. We were finally ready but, because of all my nervous outfit changing, we were going to be late.

As we sped to the restaurant, our minds were filled with questions: How would we act? What do we ask them? What will they think? What do they *want* to see in us? Will they approve of us based on this one meeting to raise their baby as our own?

It felt like we were about to be interviewed for the most important job of our lives. We had to be ourselves, yet we didn't want to put them off. We had no idea what they valued or what they were looking for. What if our love for God made them feel we were too religious? What if *not* saying we loved God made them feel we were unspiritual? What if our accomplishments in life made them feel inadequate, but what if *not* sharing our accomplishments made them worry their son wouldn't be provided for in the way they wanted?

The birth parents and Hope were already in the restaurant waiting for us. We walked in—it was a casual chain eatery where we'd all be comfortable—and Hope greeted us at the entrance. My nerves started to subside; I knew she was our advocate. Laura and Jonathan (the bio-dad) were in the back room, seated at a table. I was relieved that it was somewhat private. I didn't need onlookers making me even more nervous. Hope started the conversation and, thankfully, it began to flow easily. Oscar is a pro at talking to people. He could talk to any stranger for five minutes and you'd think they'd known each other for years.

Laura and Jonathan were quiet at first, and that's when it hit me: they were probably as nervous as we were. They were young, in their early twenties. We asked them about their lives together: how they met, what they were interested in. In fact, we ended up asking them more questions than they asked us. We found Laura to be kind, level-headed, and directed. It seemed that once she made up her mind about something—particularly adoption—there was no swaying her. I liked that.

It gave me confidence in her decision to place her baby with us.

As our lunch came to an end, we all stood up from the table. This was the first time we'd seen Laura standing up. She barely looked pregnant! Oscar and I must have looked directly at her belly with wide eyes, because Hope prompted her to unzip her hoody so we could get a glimpse of where our little baby had been hanging out the last eight months. Laura's pregnant tummy was so small for her being eight months along, and I cringed to think she was eager to get this child out of her body. *Hang on, little baby! Just a few more weeks!* I mentally encouraged our Benjamin.

Elle, Sydney, and Julia had been chosen and now they awaited the birth. Those able to form a kind of friendship with the birth mom, waited together with her. She was the conduit to their child, and they were mildly obsessed with her. And each day brought all four women closer to the event that would change the lives of everyone in this expanding web of connections, forever.

Elle

That first call with Rachel—and, in fact, on all our calls—I didn't ask invasive questions. I let her share with me what she wanted to share. This turned out to be not very much personal stuff. Mostly, our talks were about issues like: When is the baby going to be born? What is the status of the baby's health? I wanted to know everything—but it just wasn't going to be that way. Rachel was clearly in a reserved space to protect herself from feeling any more hurt than she had already suffered.

My impression of Rachel from our first conversation was that she was absolutely lovely: soft-spoken, educated, calm, and together. In fact, in all our calls and texts, Rachel exuded tremendous strength and wisdom way beyond someone her age (twenty-three—there's that lucky number again). During that period, I began to feel the utmost respect and even motherly love for her—I wanted to love on her and make all her problems go away… actually, I still do. In fact, half the time, I felt *Rachel* was counseling *me*, telling me everything was meant to be and would be okay—that this baby she was about to give birth to was really my baby and that she was just the carrier.

The only thing she did that drove me nuts was to go dark for days—a day without hearing from Rachel felt like a decade. I played super-cool and forced myself to give her all the space she needed. Literally, we were dating. I was the psycho girl not sure of the relationship. Rachel was the super-cool dude who sometimes called when she said she would and sometimes didn't. This dynamic really put me on some super-high highs and super-low lows… again, like a dating relationship.

This month, ending when we took our baby home from the hospital, was the most emotionally insane joyride of my whole entire life. The coolest day of this waiting period was when Rachel shared with me the results of her very first ultrasound (taken at month eight). She'd told me she didn't want to know the sex of the baby before she delivered because she didn't want to get attached.

So, on May 5, I anxiously called Rachel to find out the results. I asked how everything went, and with a matter-of-fact, reporter-like tone, she said, "The doctor says she looks healthy and on schedule for a delivery the third week of May." I gasped and gleefully said, "OMG!!! Did you just say 'she'?" This call was one of the most exciting moments of my life—the dream was becoming more real every second. I was to have a daughter! Wow!

Sydney

After years of waiting, everything was suddenly lining up fast, and the reality of a baby was coming to life. Every ticking moment was a balance between getting our home ready and staying close to Quinn. I woke up many mornings with new excitement and ideas for gifts to shower her with. I couldn't help wanting to give to her, even though all my thoughtful and clever ideas couldn't hold a candle to the gift she was giving us.

My gifts—after the first semi-fiasco of giving her makeup she wouldn't wear—became a fun endeavor. On our second visit, we went to her doctor appointment and had lunch, and I gave her a set of candles with a note that said: "A lit candle is an emblematic icon for hope, love, joy, passion, and security, but also sorrow. May each candle be lit and symbolize faith, serenity, and freedom as we share this soulful journey together. We will be forever grateful for your humility and graciousness in making this enduring decision."

For our third visit, I created a birth mom journal for Quinn. I Googled birth moms' stories, printed them out, and pasted them into a journal with enough extra pages for her to add her own thoughts. She told me she was going to write a letter to Cole explaining why she had made this choice for him. I don't know if she read the journal, because we never got a letter from her. All that really mattered was that she knew the journal gift came from the heart and that she was important to us.

All our doctor visits were so comfortable. After seeing the doctor, we'd eat lunch and hang out, getting to know each other better. I learned that her brother had been adopted into another family out of foster care. I also heard more about the biological dad. Though it wasn't all positive, I know it was a situation any teen girl on a mission to get married could get into. I continued to praise her for being mature and wise by placing her baby in a home that could provide for the child, since she couldn't. Her confidence level and commitment to going through with it was reassuring. It seemed, at times, too good to be true.

Julia

Oscar and I walked away from our lunch with Laura and Jonathan, the biological parents, feeling that, although we'd all gotten along well, we didn't have any deeper understanding of them.

Oscar, especially, wondered what the parents were really like. From watching his older boys grow up, he knew that raising a child was a constant process of discovery. He could see different pieces of himself in everything they did. He wanted to be able to share with our own son that he is a wonderful combination of elements from his biological parents and the things that *we* would give him and teach him. Consequently, there was no end to what he wanted to know about the birth parents. Oscar could have spent days with Laura and Jonathan, getting to know them. Since that was impossible, he wished they could have told him in that one hour every passion, every challenge, every joy, every frustration they'd ever experienced. That way, he might share with our child why it is that he loves certain things and can't stand others.

When Oscar had asked what their favorite subjects were in school, they both said, "Lunch!" He and I felt disappointed. We'd had only had a limited time frame (lunch!) to get to know them, so it was hard to tell if they were being understandably guarded or if that breezy reply revealed the true depth of them.

After lunch, we had a few hours before our flight left Sacramento. Feeling the enormous relief of making it through our meeting without any major mishaps, we decided to kill some time by relaxing with a beer and doing a little shopping. We didn't yet know their impressions of us, so there was a lingering uncertainty. Mostly, we felt relief. We liked them and felt the meeting had gone well.

After a quick drink, we wandered aimlessly through a nearby mall, anxiously waiting to hear from Hope after she dropped Laura off. When my phone finally rang, Hope had good news. She said they both really liked us and were even more confident in their decision to place their baby with us!

It was amazing to imagine we were their first choice. After all we had been through—years of hoping and of trying—it was too much to believe. We held each other and smiled. But deep down inside, I wondered if this might be just one more time our hopes would be dashed. Getting pregnant through IVF had created such hope, such expectation, and so much joy… then to get the news that we had lost the baby was a crushing blow. There were things we did not speak about, even to one another. Those were fears and pain left best to ourselves. And now the possibility of joy was so close, we could not really release any of the pent-up emotions within us. "What if…" is the most accurate description of what we felt.

The plane ride home was an adventure in itself. The wind was blowing over the mountains at 80 to 100 miles per hour, and our relatively small plane was pitching horribly left and right. Each gust sent us up over one hundred feet, then dropped us like a rock. On approach, the lady in front of us threw up. People were crying. I was squeezing Oscar's hand. You could see the lights of the runway in front of us, but the plane would not stay on course. One second we were too high, then pushed down to where our approach was too steep, and then we jerked left and right. We had already made a huge circle waiting for the wind to die down, but to no avail. The pilot continued—we all hoped he knew what he was doing. Just as we descended to about one hundred feet above the runway, the plane hit turbulence and up we went again. The pilot immediately aborted the approach and turned radically to the right as he hit the throttle.

Here we were—*the chosen ones*, about to be the parents of a little bundle of joy—and yet, again, we were reminded that life is so fragile. We were only people being tossed about helplessly in a tiny plane.

On the second approach, the pilot somehow managed to land the plane. As we were departing, a passenger in front of us thanked the flight attendant. The attendant laughed and said, motioning to the pilot, "You should be thanking him; I was just praying like the rest of you." *God had answered our prayers one more time. Hope would not disappoint us. Just as He saw us through this storm, He was about to open the windows of heaven and give us the greatest blessing of all. My dream of being a mom was so close… and now I began to truly believe that hope would not disappoint us.*

That day was the only time we had contact with Laura before the birth. I received updates from Hope about doctor appointments and the like, but we had very little time to connect further. Two weeks later we got the call: Laura was in labor!

Ginger

A few weeks after my call with Amber never happened, our adoption attorney, Melinda, called us. Amber was in labor.

While I was on the phone with Melinda, her cell phone rang with a call from a friend of Amber's. The baby had just arrived at 11:13 p.m., eastern time. She weighed six pounds and four ounces. A girl! I didn't even take a moment to think. I yelled to Gordon, "Call United and book a flight to Ohio!" Since Amber was considering us to be adoptive parents, Gordon and I agreed it was best to be present, for her and for the baby. I took a red-eye flight across the country.

Looking back, I realize how nerve-racking that whole experience could have been. But, actually, it wasn't. I had such clarity that this was the right thing to do. Where there had been chaos before, everything began to fall into place. My only challenge was trying to sleep on the plane while thinking about the baby girl I was about to meet!

There was another concern, a much more serious one. Melinda told us that Amber had thrown a big party one weekend and was concerned that the hospital would test her for drug use. *I tried to swallow my resentment toward a woman who would use during pregnancy.* When I was pregnant with my son, I would hold my breath if I walked by someone who was smoking. And here was a woman who took who-knows-what while she was pregnant. We'd been told there was no drug use up to this point in the pregnancy, but I kept hearing my son's pediatrician's voice in my head: "Birth mothers lie. If she says it was just one time, that is a lie." It was tough to swallow, but he had seen many situations that justified this statement.

The next morning, I went straight from the airport to the hospital. Melinda had told Amber I would be coming. But I hadn't heard any feedback, so I felt a bit like an uninvited guest. And quite frankly, I wanted to learn of any drug-related concerns. My goal was to be open and warm and comforting, and hopefully get a signal from Amber as to her intentions about placement.

I remember thinking as I waited outside her hospital room, *Life will be totally different after I walk through this door . . .*

Chapter ♡ Five
A Labor of Love

Adoption counselors and attorneys had given Ginger, Elle, Sydney, and Julia a nice, orderly, step-by-step playbook for labor, birth, and the aftermath at the hospital. It was just a matter of following the steps, right? No way. When the time came, the steps were tossed out, everything was improvised on the spot, and they were operating on gut. But, interestingly enough, it was okay. Any confusion or tension was erased from their minds by the first glimpse of their babies, and by the magical moment when someone—a nurse, maybe—casually referred to them as the "mother" and "father."

Ginger

We had been enjoying Labor Day weekend with our three-year-old son, and then I was in Ohio at a hospital, about to meet a woman who had just given birth to a girl who might become our daughter.

Waiting to meet Amber, I was stressing myself out, overthinking the meeting. What should I say? What was *she* thinking? I was set to focus on being sympathetic, as if I were going to see an acquaintance who had just given birth… "friend" seemed a little too intimate at this point. I had a nice bouquet of flowers from the gift shop and was ready to go. As I waited outside her door, a hospital administrator said I couldn't go in until a social worker arrived. *No problem, fair enough*, I thought. I was playing by their rules. I had waited for years—what difference would a couple more minutes make? My flowers and I headed back to the waiting room.

At that point I really felt unwelcome. Had I made the right decision to come out here? She might turn me away, and I'd be back on a flight home that night. I was so glad no one but Gordon knew I was here. I learned the hard way, after too many failed IVF cycles, to keep lips zipped until I was certain there was real news to share. Why should others experience the angst and disappointment?

Chill, Ginger, I said to myself. I had to accept that this was a part of my life where I had little control. I coached myself: *Take a deep breath and wait to see what happens next.*

Two *People* magazine issues later, out came the hospital administrator and the social worker. *Be polite,* I reminded myself. *They are just doing their job.* They asked why I was there. I gave a high-level overview of the story. I could only imagine how they saw me—woman flies in from California hoping to pick up a baby. I tried to use my soft voice, explaining that I wasn't familiar with hospital regulations, that this was all completely foreign to me. I offered to connect them with my attorney, Melinda, if that would help.

They explained that Amber had delivered around eleven p.m. the previous night and hadn't yet spoken with a social worker. That was the next step, to confirm she was okay meeting with me. I conveyed kindness. *I come in peace… I am not a threat,* I silently beamed at the two women, as I smiled and said, "Of course; I completely understand." The fact was Melinda, my adoption attorney, had told Amber I was coming. But the hospital hadn't been notified, and a social worker needed to speak with her before she met any prospective parents. My guess is that this rule is meant to protect the birth mother at a particularly vulnerable moment from any pressure to place her baby. That completely made sense to me.

Fifteen minutes later, they returned to say I could go in to meet Amber. I'd hoped for some hint about Amber's position on placing, but no additional information was given.

Okay, my flowers and I headed back to the door. I heard her on the phone, so I walked the hall. How many times was I going to have to psych myself up for this introduction? Finally, there was silence from within the room, and I knocked. She said, "Come in…"

Amber was laying in bed, a petite blonde woman with a great smile. Oh, how wonderful to be greeted with a smile! Her first words to me were, "Have you seen her?" Those were the sentiments I was looking for—she was pleased I was there, and she wanted me to see the baby. A good start.

"No," I answered. "I wanted to meet you first." I was thinking, *They wouldn't even let me see you, so I'm sure seeing the baby would've been a no-no.* "Oh, I'll have them bring her in." I asked her how she was feeling, how her labor had gone. She said she was okay, but she was tired and had a cold. The hospital wouldn't turn the air down in her room. There were photos of the baby, taken by the hospital, scattered around the bed. How interesting that I would see a *photo* of the baby before seeing *her*.

"I told them to wait on ordering the photos until you got here," Amber said. Then a woman came in with order forms. This was telling me something. Now I was ordering photos of the baby, literally picking from packages A through E, with options for magnets, coffee mugs, and even announcements. It was a surreal experience, but I continued to say to myself, *just go with it.* All the pieces were falling into place.

Then they brought in the baby, and Amber let me hold her—oh my, what an angel! She had a peaceful face, rosebud lips, and an adorable cleft in her chin. Amber said her grandmother had a cleft chin—now I wish I had a picture of her grandmother to show Olivia! We sat and chatted and stared at the baby. From that moment, I called her Baby. I had a girl's name in mind, but I wasn't ready to even think of her with that name for fear that she wouldn't be going home with me. When Amber wanted to nap, I stepped out and called Gordon, overwhelmed with news of what might be—in fact, would *probably* be—our baby girl! This was look-ing more and more like a reality. Together, we celebrated with cautious optimism. We started making plans for Gordon to fly out later in the week.

Then, in the hallway, a nurse pulled me aside to tell me that Baby was born with drugs in her system. This comment was probably a violation of some code in the hospital's manual on engagement, but I so appreciated her honesty. Because of what Melinda had told me, this was not a complete surprise. The bigger question was what else had taken place in the last nine months? We would never know the answer to that question. This was one of our many leaps of faith throughout the adoption process.

Later that day, I met with the hospital administrator and social worker, who told me Amber would be released from the hospital the next day, but that Baby would remain in the hospital. In Ohio, a four-day period is required between labor and relinquishment of the birth mother's rights. I didn't have any facts or studies to back this up, but I intuitively knew that if Baby was going to thrive, she needed love and nurturing above and beyond the basic feeding and changing by nursing staff from Day One of her life. *Who was going to rock her and nuzzle her? Who was going to sing to her? Who was going to mother her?* Thank goodness the hospital administrators listened and were supportive. They offered me a room in the hospital and access to the nursery until final arrangements were made. Good for Baby, good for me.

Sydney

During the third week of doctor visits, Quinn and I went to together. The ques-tion we faced was, "Should we induce?" The doctor looked at both of us and said, "The baby is over nine pounds, and Quinn is ready." Quinn turned to me to make the choice. I thought about how, in twenty-four hours, the baby could possibly be born on the date both Quinn's parents said would be bad, because they had jobs they couldn't leave. Yikes. But I said, "Yes, let's do it," knowing that July 17 was the due date I'd hoped for and that it would be just as special and lucky as 07/07/07, our wedding day. Phillip and I committed to staying with Quinn the day she'd be induced, so she wouldn't be alone if she went into labor.

We met her family for lunch and shared the appointment details. Although they weren't happy that we chose a day neither could leave their jobs, we came up with a plan to make it work. Phillip and I arranged to stay at a hotel directly across the street from where Cole would be born. Quinn stayed with her dad that night. We all said our good-byes, knowing what the next day would bring.

We woke up at six forty-five a.m. to a text from Quinn saying, "I am in labor," and boy was she. Her dad had rushed her to the hospital just in time to get her checked in and start heavy labor. Meanwhile, Phillip and I were taking our time, after Hope, the facilitator, told us to relax, get breakfast, and be prepared to wait all day. We were following these instructions until a frantic call came from Quinn's dad, telling us to hurry up and get there, that the baby was coming. The best thing was that the labor was going fast and it was early morning, so both her parents could be with Quinn as she gave birth, before they had to be at work.

Rushing to the labor and delivery area of the hospital, I heard the loudest screaming voice shout, "Get this baby out of me!" This was followed up by every profane term you can image someone in labor yelling. I looked at Phillip tearfully and said, "That's Quinn; come on." We were rushed through swinging doors by a doctor who said, "Your daughter knows how to deliver a baby," and we said, "She's not our daughter, but she's having our baby; we are adopting." As we almost ran with the doctor to Quinn's room, we asked breathlessly, "Did she have it?" to which he curtly replied, "No, but she is about to."

That was the beginning of the dance. What I mean by "dance" is that, while we were all together at the hospital, Phillip and I were trying our best to be sensitive to Quinn's emotions, and to handle every situation with her delicately. It was an improvised dance—invented on the spot— because *nothing* was occurring the way we'd been led to expect in our adoption workshops. Our adoption counselor had described the usual steps: You will wait to be asked into the labor room; you will let the birth mom hold the baby first; you will let the birth mom have her own time with the baby right after they clean her up and bring her back to the mom's room; and the hospital will be informed that this is an open adoption by a protocol letter sent ahead of the birth.

All of this was opposite what we'd worked out with Quinn and what had actually happened at the hospital.

Quinn told us ahead of time she wanted her parents, Hope, Phillip, and me there during delivery. Her only rule was that Phillip and her dad stay at the head of the bed, but she winked at me and said, "I don't care what *you* see, Sydney." She asked if we wanted to hold him first and we told her it was her choice, and she agreed to have him put on her first and then passed to me.

We never determined who was going to cut the umbilical cord until one hour and thirty-nine minutes into it. Building up to that point were the most intense moments in our lives! We watched a team of doctors run in and out while I held the hand and cradled Quinn's forehead as she labored through the epidural-free (there had been no time to give this) birth of a 9.2-pound baby. Looking back and forth at her father standing off to the side so we could be a part of this joyous moment, watching the clock and the heart monitor and wondering when Hope and Quinn's mom would arrive: this was the longest time of my life. Countdown to delivery was spent encouraging Quinn to breathe through the contractions and controlling her need to shout out, "I want a C-section!" and helping through the moments when she nearly passed out, moaning, "I can't push anymore." Sweaty palms, tearful eyes, excitement, worry, and strength all played a role during delivery.

Over an hour into it, just when Quinn was getting weaker and not wanting to put the effort into delivery, her mom and Hope arrived. At that point, she became despondent and angry, and the intensity was worsening for all of us. There was nothing any of us could do that suited her. She even slapped me off her a few times, but I wasn't taking it personally. I was there to take all pain and suffering away from her, and if being her punching bag was helping, then I would be it!

I never imagined having this up close and personal experience of labor and delivery through adoption. Being by Quinn's side while she bore down to deliver a child that was going to be placed in our life was both overwhelming and gratifying.

However, our joy quickly shifted when the baby's heart monitor showed signs of stress. "One strong push and the baby could be out," we all chanted. "Come on, Quinn, you can do it!" And then suddenly, the look on the doctors' faces forced all of us to stop our cheerleading and see that Cole was coming out "sunny side up." I never knew what this term meant except for ordering eggs for breakfast, and sure enough, Cole was coming out facing up, rather than down. This was the most emotionally bonding moment of our lives for all of us. We will never forget the next words spoken in the delivery room: "Who will cut the cord?" As the tears streamed down all our faces, we looked at Phillip and said, "His dad will."

Elle

I was beyond excited to meet Rachel face to face before she gave birth, but I didn't want to force anything on her that she wasn't comfortable with. I was given an approximate due week; I had to figure out when to fly out to the Big Apple. The Friday night before I left San Francisco for my friends' apartment in Manhattan, I gave Rachel a heads-up text telling her I was flying into NYC.

When it's a case of adoption at birth, the hospital asks the biological mother to respond on a form to sensitive questions:

1. During labor, who do you want in the room?
2. During delivery, who would you like with you?
3. When the baby is born, do you want to be first to hold the baby, or not see the baby at all?
4. Do you want to spend time alone with the baby?
5. Do you want to name the baby, or should the adoptive parents?

The only question Rachel answered was number two. She wanted her mom in the delivery room with her. All her answers to the other questions were a big fat mystery to me, and this really made me anxious.

Driving to the airport that Saturday morning, I kept thinking about how crazy it was that I'd be meeting my baby girl in a matter of days. My "new chapter" had officially started, and this new chapter included a hell of a lot of luggage. My bag was stuffed to the gills with cargo pants, T-shirts and workout gear—a.k.a. Mom Gear—as I didn't know how long I'd be gone. Into the baby's bag, I'd stuffed objects completely foreign to me: Pampers newborn diapers, Butt Paste, pacifiers, onesies, burp cloths, rectal thermometers, California Baby No-Tear Hair and Body Wash, Aden and Anis swaddling muslin blankets, Even-Flo bottles, Kirkland baby wipes, a Baby Bjorn, and the all-important (more for the parents than the baby) Sleep Sheep.

My second morning in Manhattan, I received a text from Rachel that said simply, "Sometime early this evening the doctor is planning to induce labor. All is well. Baby and I are healthy and we're coming down the home stretch! :)" With this text, the "dream" started to become real to me. Wow, the time had finally come!

I decided it was time to bite the bullet and go to the hospital. In the waiting room, all seats were taken, so I sat cross-legged on the floor against the wall. I texted Rachel that I was in the waiting room if she needed me and wished her luck. After many hours of waiting with no word from Rachel, I left the hospital a little after two a.m. and headed back to Manhattan.

Back in the apartment, I was so tired and yet so amped. Sleep did not come. Then a text came through from Rachel saying, "Everything's okay here. Sleeping on and off, cramping a lot now. I hope you're okay." She's hoping *I'm* okay. *Wow,* I thought, *what an amazing young woman to be worried about my well-being at a time like this, when she must be scared out of her mind and in major discomfort.* Rachel was my hero. That was the last text I got from her before the baby was born.

The next morning, as I pulled into Hertz to meet Jack and our rental SUV (to hold all the baby gear we had no idea how to use), I got a call from Deidre, Rachel's mom. Steadily, Deidre told me Rachel was officially in labor and that things were going smoothly. Off the phone, I united with Jack and it was breathtaking. Nothing can prepare you for seeing your significant other with a carseat and snap-and-go stroller for the first time. I'll never forget how completely *hot* Jack looked carrying all this baby gear to the rental car. It was a complete turn-on for me—pure porn. I still smile thinking back on that moment (sigh).

Then, while Jack and I were bantering about which coffee shop to stop into to get our cup o' joe, my cell phone rang with Rachel's name flashing on the screen, silently screaming, telling me "Pɪᴄᴋ ᴜᴘ!" I answered a call that would forever change everything. It was Deidre: "Elle, I'm calling to congratulate you and Jack on your new baby girl. She is absolutely perfect. In fact, she's beautiful! Rachel did absolutely great. It happened very fast, and she is recovering easily."

With that, I hung up and looked over at my copilot; giddy with excitement, I exclaimed, "Congratulations, Daddy!!! Our baby girl was just born a few minutes ago at 8:28 a.m. Let's ditch that coffee and go meet our new baby girl!"

As Jack and I rushed from the car and headed into the hospital, I was without a doubt the most complete and utter nervous wreck that I'd ever been in my thirty-nine years. A nurse took us to Rachel and the baby in recovery, and I now know what an "out-of-body" experience is, because I had one when the nurse pushed the last door open. There was a beaming Rachel sitting proudly, upright in her bed, cradling her (and the biological dad's) beautiful creation… our (not quite yet) angel baby girl. She was finally here!

Overcome with emotion for what Rachel had just gone through and unselfishly brought into my and Jack's life, I rushed to Rachel and took her sweet face in my hands and kissed it tenderly. Not wanting to let go of her—and for some unexplainable reason not being ready to look at the baby—I hugged her and buried my sprouting tears in her sandy blonde hair. Rachel was smiling at me in such a heartfelt way, and I couldn't even begin to explain to her at that moment in front of her mom and dad and Jack how happy yet sad I felt for her. I wanted to erase all the pain that was behind her big smile. I wanted to take care of and nurture not only this new precious baby she had in her arms, but also *her*.

Finally letting go of Rachel, I drank in the sight of the baby she was cradling in her arms. Without missing a beat, Rachel offered the swaddled little nugget to me and I deferred the precious bundle to Jack, who scooped her up and declared, "Hi there, you! You are our Golden Nugget."

Watching Jack hold the baby was so amazingly beautiful. Then I walked over to the other side of the bed and hugged and kissed Rachel's parents, Deidre and Sam, who declared, "We know what you are going through right now… we went through the exact same thing twenty-three years ago." (Yes, Rachel had come to them through adoption.) Jack handed me the baby. Oh, wow, what an amazing moment! I was so nervous and excited and cautious, devouring my first sight of this little nugget in my arms… I drank in her beautifully articulated features, pouty red lips, thick black hair and perfect fingers and toes. I was in complete awe and disbelief that here she was… our baby was finally here!

Rachel asked me what her name was, and I said, "What do you think of Harper?" She and Deidre quickly declared they loved that name. A minute later, a nurse hurried in to get the baby cleaned up and checked into the nursery.

Julia

It was two-and-a-half weeks before Laura was due. I was at a movie with my girlfriends, and Oscar was at a hockey game with his sons. I'd begun carrying my phone in my pocket everywhere I went, anticipating "the Call" at any time. An hour into the movie, my phone vibrated. It was Hope. I ran out of the theater, leaving my friends behind and called Oscar. "It's time! Laura's in labor!"

We rushed home and packed our bags, including one for little Benjamin. We were on the road in half an hour! The all-night drive from Colorado to California seemed impossibly long. We were sure we wouldn't make it to the hospital in time for the birth, but we wanted to be there as soon as possible. For me, we couldn't get there fast enough even if it was just across town! I felt like a kid in the back of the car on a long drive to vacation: "Are we there yet?"

All the excitement, all the emotion, was taking a toll on our energy. It was very late in the evening when we started, and by midnight we were only four hours into an eighteen-hour drive. We got a text that her labor had stopped. *What did that mean?* we wondered. Would they send her home? Was this not really "it"? Oscar and I decided to pull off into a motel and sleep for a few hours. We figured by the time we got up, we'd know if they had sent her home and we should turn around, or if her labor had progressed and we should keep on our way.

Five a.m. came quickly. We got a text that Laura had given birth two hours earlier and that there were problems. Benjamin wasn't breathing on his own and had to be transferred to another hospital with a neonatal intensive care unit. We had so many fears and questions as we sped through the breaking dawn toward our new son. Was he going to be okay? Would he need extended care? Or worse… would he even make it?

We received a few short texts from Laura and the biological dad, Jonathan, through the day as we drove. They had gone to the other hospital with the baby. There was a limited exchange of information and one worrisome photo texted to us of Benjamin attached to various tubes and machines. His tiny body was struggling through the first hours of his life. The lack of real medical information on his status and the lone photo didn't ease our fears. I texted other family and friends through the day, asking for prayers, updating our location, and giving what little info we had on Benjamin.

Sydney texted often, concerned about how I was doing; she offered words of encouragement. I'm sure she understood both the excitement and anxiety I was feeling. It was reassuring to me to have a friend who knew exactly what I was going through at this moment.

As we neared Sacramento, my anxieties heightened. Not for fear of Benjamin's health, but about something I had never considered: *I was about to meet my son for the first time.* We were total strangers and about to be joined together for life. It was so different from having nine months to bond with a baby in your womb. Maybe it's similar to meeting your husband for the first time in an arranged marriage. Will he like me? Will I like him? I knew these were silly questions. Just because I was adopting my son didn't make the bond any less strong. But I couldn't help playing out these fears in my head. The only person I knew who may have ever felt the same was Sydney. All my other friends had been blessed with fertility, and so I felt a special connection to her as she guided and mentored me through the adoption process.

We were getting closer. Oscar and I were speeding down into the Sacramento area out of the Sierra Mountains. It seemed that the closer we got to the hospital, the stronger my anxieties grew. I sent Sydney a text, hoping she would give me some sort of encouragement or wisdom from her own experience. As I hit "send," I looked up through the windshield and saw the most incredible thing.

"Speed up!" I told Oscar.

"What? Why?" We were already going pretty fast. Traffic in all four lanes speeding into the city was barely keeping up with us.

"That's *Sydney's car!*" I said, pointing to a one about two car lengths ahead of us. I knew it was hers from the peace sign sticker in the window. It was her signature.

"No way," Oscar said. But I knew. As we pulled up alongside her car and honked the horn, Phillip looked over from the driver's seat and dropped his jaw. We pulled off together at the next exit.

This all seemed so improbable! The chances of us running into Phillip and Sydney—on an eight-lane freeway... on our way to meet our son... after driving for sixteen hours—were next to nothing!

Phillip and Sydney had been with us from the very beginning of our adoption journey. They'd encouraged us to enter the process after they adopted sweet Cole, and Sydney had supported me through all the ups and downs. That evening, alongside the highway on the way to meet our son, and amid hugs, tears, and laughter, many of my anxieties were put to rest.

It was evident that God had orchestrated this. I know he put Sydney in my life to encourage me through the journey toward my long-awaited child. From the day we met, when I learned of her own fertility struggles, to this chance meeting on the side of the road, I knew I had a special friend with whom I could share my thoughts, fears, and struggles. I wasn't alone in this journey to my son. This was one more way God was reminding me of that.

Oscar and I arrived at the hospital twelve hours after Benjamin was born. We pulled into the parking garage, found the closest parking spot and rushed into the hospital. We navigated our way to the elevators that led to the NICU, uncertain what we would find a floor above. We hadn't received any status reports from Jonathan or Laura in several hours. The elevator doors creaked open on the second floor, and we entered the waiting room. There, Jonathan sat tiredly, slouched in a chair. When he saw us, he quickly sat up and gestured to someone lying on a bench next to him. "They're here!" he said abruptly.

That was when we realized the sleeping person was Laura. She'd been waiting there for us all day. We later learned she'd left the hospital three hours after giving birth to travel with Benjamin to the NICU across town. Because she had checked herself out of the first hospital, they wouldn't give her a room in the second. So she'd had to wait in the waiting room for nine more hours until we arrived. She told us she didn't want him to be alone as he waited for his parents to get there. His parents. *His parents.* That was us! This was the first time that I really felt like he was ours.

Laura gave us both a hug and asked how our trip was. She was obviously exhausted but ready to introduce us to our son. She took us to the door of the NICU, where we were allowed in. While we scrubbed, she told the nurse manning the door that we were his parents and would be there at the hospital for him.

We approached his bed. There he was. Our son. He was beautiful. Precious. Tiny. Even though he was only two-and-a-half weeks early, he was very small. He was only five pounds, four ounces. Even though he was connected to various tubes and monitors, I could see all his features. His small face looked so round and perfect—not like most newborns. He had a small button nose, a pink mouth, and his head was covered in a fine blonde fuzz. I was instantly in love.

Both Laura and I stood looking at him for a while in silence. We both touched his tiny hands and feet. I cupped his little head with the palm of my hand. I was in awe. I was overjoyed. I wondered what Laura's heart was going through. This was the culmination of a dream I'd had for so long. But how was she going to start over after today? There was no way to ask her these questions now. Maybe not ever.

We met with the doctors. They said Benjamin was going to be okay. His breathing had been regulated; however, they wanted him to stay in the hospital for a week.

Obviously exhausted, Laura hugged Oscar and me. Then she said she wanted to give us time and space to get to know our boy. She would be back later in the week to say good-bye, and then she went home to rest.

After they left, Oscar and I stood over our son… for the first time. We were a family.

During those fleeting days in the hospital after the birth, while they were bonding with their babies, Julia, Elle, Ginger, and Sydney were keenly aware that the biological mother was saying good-bye to the same child. How could they spare the birth moms this sadness, they wondered? The answer was they couldn't. Filled with this surging, never-before-felt love for their children, fully capable of happily staring for hours at their babies' features, they could only express your gratitude to the biological mother. Again. And again.

Julia

That first night, Oscar and I just stared at Benjamin endlessly. It was almost midnight before we returned home to Oscar's parents' house. We were so blessed that our son was not only born near them, but also in the same hospital as Oscar's father, his two brothers, and sister had been born! We were glad to have a comfortable place to stay, as it was up in the air when Benjamin would be released from the hospital.

That night, before we left, the nurses encouraged us to come back early for his first feeding and diaper change. They knew the journey we were on, and seemed to want to do everything they could to help along the bonding process.

The next morning, I made sure to be there for our son's breakfast, stayed through his lunch, and then returned to the hospital for his late-night bottle. We got to bathe him, change him, and check his temperature and weight. I wanted to spend every moment with him.

The second morning we were there, Oscar and I got to have our first skin-to-skin contact. For the first time, Benjamin was allowed outside his hospital bassinet that so closely monitored all his vital signs. I remember reclining in the chair, holding Benjamin's tiny body against my chest. It was so dark and quiet in the nursery that the only noise was the beeping of his heart monitor. Because he was so small, his heart raced at erratic intervals. I watched the monitor, tracking the pace. The most wonderful thing happened a few minutes after we were sitting together. His heart rate slowed and steadied. His small head rested on my chest, tilted upward. He was so content that his mouth gaped open as he slept. *It was as if he knew I was his mommy.* And the complete peace I felt in my heart confirmed that he was my son.

On the fourth day, Oscar had to return home to Colorado to finish up a project. It was important for him to continue his work and keep his clients happy. We were both determined to keep our businesses up and running amid this life change.

The afternoon he left, we met with Laura and Jonathan to sign relinquishment papers. There was a certainty in their mind-set that gave me peace. We all knew this was the best decision for our son. The four parents sat in a tiny room off the NICU with the social worker. She was brief yet compassionate. First the signatures, then the photocopies, and it was done. Laura and Jonathan wanted to see Benjamin. I walked them into his room and left them there to say good-bye. Oscar and I waited in the hallway. Jonathan came out first; shortly afterward, Laura emerged. I wondered what she was feeling. From knowing her even briefly, I knew she wasn't one to wear her emotions on her sleeve. She was a strong girl and, even though she may have been hurting, it wasn't evident.

Afterward, all four of us met up with Hope for lunch. Even though it was not Laura's final good-bye to Benjamin, it was our opportunity to express our gratitude to them for the amazing gift they were giving us. Oscar and I had prepared a card for her, telling her how grateful we were for her decision, and how much we would love and care for Benjamin as our son. We wanted her to know she would never have to worry about him being loved and cared for. I also gave Laura a necklace that symbolized my hope for her. It had three charms: "Live," "Laugh," and "Love." We hoped that in her future, she would live her life to the fullest, find joy in every circumstance, and continue to love.

The next day, after Oscar was back in Colorado, I spent my usual time with Benjamin: an early visit and I would stay until lunch. It wasn't until I returned to my car in the parking garage that I realized my wedding ring was gone. I'd taken it off as I scrubbed in at the NICU and had placed it in the back pocket of my jeans. Somewhere along the way, it had fallen out. I retraced my steps—all the way back inside, up the elevator, down the hall, back to Benjamin's room. I told the nurse who was on duty. She helped me search the room, the rocking chair, and even his bed. We looked in the dirty linen hamper, pulling out every blanket and sheet. We searched the diaper pail. The only other place I'd been was the bathroom. One of the nurses even put gloves on and helped me search through the trash in there!

It was gone. I couldn't believe it. My ring finger felt naked, empty, too light. I felt the absence of something that had been there for so many years. It reminded me of that hole in my heart that had just been filled. My loss paled in comparison to my gain.

Ginger

During the next day and a half, friends of Amber came to see her and bring gifts for the baby. Seeing their exchanges with Amber and Baby, I sensed their emotions as a balance between happiness for this new life full of possibilities, and overwhelming sadness that Amber would not be parenting. But how loving and thoughtful it was that they brought Baby gifts; even to this day she sleeps with one of the pink blankets she was given.

On the day she left the hospital, Amber had some time alone with the baby. I can only imagine what it must have been like to give birth and then, a day and a half later, to leave the hospital without her child. I can only guess how it felt to look at your baby and realize you are entrusting another mom to parent her.

Although nothing was official yet, and the relinquishment paperwork hadn't been signed, it was clear Amber would probably place Baby with us. I told Amber how much I appreciated the opportunity to get to know her, and that we would not let her down; if she chose to place Baby with us, we would love and take care of her forever.

When I said good-bye, it was with the understanding that I'd see Amber later in the week to introduce her to Gordon. Unfortunately, that was not to be. Amber resisted our attempts to connect with reasons (excuses, really) why she couldn't meet up.

While I'd been frantically packing to fly out to Ohio to meet Amber and Baby, I'd had a moment of total clarity. I realized I wanted to bring a meaningful gift for Amber, something with significance and sentimental value. I had two pairs of diamond earrings. (They were nothing of great value—just diamond chips really—but one pair had been given to me by Gordon's mother and my mother had given me the other. They were definitely meaningful.) I decided to keep one and give one to Amber. It didn't seem right to give the gift in the hospital—in fact, it may have been seen as inappropriate, given that Amber hadn't yet relinquished. I planned to give her the earrings when we met later in the week but, sadly, I never got the chance. I now plan to give them to my daughter.

I regret that Amber and Gordon didn't meet each other, but I understood that it was probably too much for her. Most of all, I was sorry I didn't have another opportunity to thank Amber. I hoped she was getting the support she needed. I was caring for Baby, but who was caring for Amber?

The four days when I was living in the hospital were amazing. I missed Gordon and Ethan, but I savored the bonding time I had with her. I met the maternity nurses, who made me feel so at home and welcomed me into the nursery. What an experience for a woman who had been yearning for a baby for years to then be submerged in a hospital nursery… talk about too much of a good thing! I spent every moment with Baby, feeding her, changing her, and constantly cuddling her. I'd forgotten a lot in the three-and-a-half years since Ethan was an infant, and the nurses lovingly reminded me how to care for Baby: at bedtime, put her on her back, not tummy; wash cleanest to dirtiest at bathtime; burp by rubbing, not patting; and, a new one for me as I was used to changing a boy, clean up a dirty bottom front to back. I felt like I was surrounded by loving aunts and uncles who were all supporting me.

During the stay I grew very close to the nurses. The head nurse, Suzanne, was my fairy godmother… very nurturing. She showed me compassion when I really needed it. One night I held Baby, gazing in wonder at her precious face, and said to Suzanne, "Can you imagine being pregnant with this angel and taking drugs?" I expected an answer along the lines of, "Despicable, unimaginable, sinful." Instead, she said: "There but for the grace of God go I." I was silent. I'd heard this phrase before, yet had not grasped its true meaning until that moment. Suzanne told me about the women she had seen give birth at the central city hospital, of the generations of poverty and drug use, and how it was nearly impossible for them to rise above that situation. *If not for some sort of divine intervention, it could be me in Amber's position.* I had opportunities, circumstances, privileges that directed my outcome. How could I pass judgment without knowing the whole story, without living a life in her shoes?

Suzanne's words would have a big impact on my mind-set going forward. Amber did not think the way I thought, she did not see things as I saw them, and my normal was not her normal. This did not make her actions right, but it taught me openness.

Most caring was the lactation consultant, Linda. Surprisingly, she had an open calendar, as many moms had chosen not to nurse. I explained that I'd heard of adoptive moms breast-feeding and she was excited by the project. She was hopeful of success because I'd breast-fed my son, and she believed my body would "remember" what to do.

So I pumped every four hours to motivate a response from my body. I went online and ordered herbs and tinctures to increase milk supply. Regardless of the volume of production, Linda assured me there were bonding benefits to nursing. I'd been told by the hospital administrators that, while I was allowed to be in the nursery with Baby, I had no rights until relinquishment. In fact, I wasn't permitted to be alone with her. But in the nursery, the nurses are the bosses. The hospital was in a poor part of town, and they'd seen situations where there was no loving prospective parent to step in. They supported adoption. They understood my heartfelt desire to breast feed, and gave me a private room in the nursery for spending time with Baby. "Let's give you two some privacy," they said.

And so, in my small room, sitting in a rocking chair, I nursed and cuddled and had skin-to-skin contact with Baby. It was a miraculous time. And to think of the risk they took to help us, violating policy to give us alone time. These angels were acting in Baby's best interest, and I thank them for caring for her and for me.

Sydney

Once Cole was out and getting his stats taken, Phillip and I divided our time between checking in with Quinn and bonding with Cole. We took a zillion photos, got him changed into his going-home outfit, and then wondered *when* we would take him home.

Now the *process* of adoption became front and center. Quinn was only back in her room for a few hours when the social worker showed up, and everything became very much about "us" and "them." We were told the baby could be released to us the minute the hospital said he was safe to come home. It turned out, because of Cole's large size, they wanted to keep him a few extra days, which made things a little tense between all of us. The first day, we were all together as a family. The second and third day, we were talking as if we would only see Quinn and her parents once a year, and that sad moment when the "contact agreement" reared its head back at the Starbucks was looming over us again.

During the entire process of adoption, I could never predict any of the outcomes, either good or bad. I really wasn't prepared for labor and delivery. After it was all over, Phillip said to me, "Did you think it was going to be like this?"

I answered him, "No, did you?"

Phillip still tells the story to everyone, ending with the words, "I thought we would show up at the hospital and do the paperwork in a private area, never see our birth mom, and take the baby home." Instead, thanks to open adoption and Hope, the birth was treated as a celebration. So, for three days, that's what the dance was about.

The minute Quinn wanted food, we ordered her favorite pizza from a takeout spot. The first day and well into the night were spent in her room, loving back and forth on Quinn and Cole. Quinn took a few turns holding him when she wasn't on her iPhone, checking Facebook, or texting her friends that she'd given birth.

You could read right away there was no interest in the baby, but there was a need for attention for having given birth. Yet this first day was comfortable and open, and Quinn really wanted to celebrate. She asked why none of our family was there to visit. We told her that we didn't know how she would feel about that, and that my sister had told me she was a phone call away. Quinn said, "Call her. I want to meet her and have her meet your son."

Not only was it okay to have my sister there, it seemed Quinn might have texted the biological dad's mother and sister, with whom she still had a relationship, because a few hours after the birth they showed up. I was never so worried about a sudden shift in the wind until then. But they were gracious and gave us their best wishes, held Cole, and kissed him good-bye. They also shared positive things about the biological dad and said he just wasn't mature enough to be a dad. Kind of mind-blowing, considering he was thirty-nine, but maturity isn't determined by age, I guess.

At the end of the first day, we put Cole back into the nursery and we were all able to get a good night's sleep: Quinn in her hospital bed, and Phillip, my sister, and I across the street in a hotel.

On the second day, we woke up early to take a shower and get over to Quinn and Cole for the first feeding. But before we left the hotel, we got a frantic call from Quinn's mom, saying, "Where are you? This baby needs to eat and Quinn is getting attached." For the first time, worry that things could change crept into our minds. *Why was the baby with Quinn?* The hospital knew it was an adoption situation and was informed not to bring the baby into the birth mom's room until the adopting family was there. Unfortunately, the night shift hadn't informed the morning shift. Once we got there, everything was fine, but we felt daggers going through us from Quinn's parents. It dawned on me at that moment, we had the best gift in life—a newborn baby—and they were there with nothing but a sad daughter who would need a lot of love for the emptiness she was about to experience.

I sensed Quinn was feeling an echo of her own experience—being placed in a foster home, then adopted at an older age. How rewarding, I imagined, it must be for her to know her son would not go through any of that. In fact, there was more tension between Quinn and her parents than between Quinn and us. And I couldn't help but bond with Quinn and try to fill the void of love she wasn't receiving from her parents.

The days and hours were long, but things were getting easier. I changed Quinn's undergarments as many times as I changed Cole's diapers. Her parents were in and out for short times. We had a few highs and lows, with Quinn having pain from the delivery and suffering from a lack of attention, as I tried to stay out of her room and be in the nursery all day to bond with Cole and give Quinn the separation she needed. My sister and I had a good tag team plan, switching off with Cole and Quinn, and my sister was playing even more of a maternal role with Quinn than I was. A wise mother of four, she was succeeding in getting Quinn excited about resuming the life of a nineteen-year-old, now that she had this hurdle and obstacle out of her way. It was reassuring to know we could keep Quinn positive during the transition. By the end of the second night, we had that assurance more than ever.

That evening, as Phillip and I waited to say goodnight to Quinn, we overheard the social worker talking to her about what would happen if she changed her mind the next day. We didn't hear much more than Quinn saying, "I know and I won't." When we went to say goodnight to Quinn, we got a warm smile from the social worker and a big hug from Quinn, who said, "I love you guys, and know I'm doing the right thing for Cole." We were so relieved, although puzzled about what exactly the social worker had been saying to Quinn.

Once back at our hotel, we called Hope and explained what we'd heard. And God love Hope, she simply said, "Girl, this is the lime in your corona." I laughed and said, "What does that mean?" Hope answered, "Quinn and the bio-dad had a domestic arrest and it's on her record. The social worker was informing her that if she didn't sign over her rights, the baby would be taken by Child Protective Services." *Wow, what a blessing that the right choice was made for Cole,* was the first thing that came to our minds.

That night, I couldn't wait to go to bed and wake up to checking out of the hospital and getting home to start our family. Everything was in place at home, and our days spent in the hospital felt positive. We'd agreed on when to have our first visit with Quinn. It would be around the time of her birthday, only two-and-a-half months away.

The final step was our adoption agency releasing Cole to our custody. Just as Phillip had imagined, we were now taken off to a separate room to sign all the paperwork. Suddenly, it no longer felt like a celebration; it was back to the daunting process. And what ended the celebration was Quinn's mother barging into the room to tell our adoption agent that the baby would not be leaving the hospital before the birth mom was released. Phillip and I couldn't help but worry about why Quinn wasn't being released, only to find out she was still having pain and trouble from the delivery. Quinn's mother also told us that Quinn did not want to say good-bye to Cole but she did want to see us. I reacted instantly, telling Phillip we'd go in separately so one of us could stay with Cole.

I let Phillip go in first, and he was quick and cordial. I followed, and found Quinn and her mother lying together on Quinn's bed. I went to Quinn's side, grabbed her hand, shared tears, and gave her yet another gift. This gift was my most inspired. A few weeks before Cole was born, at a little store, I'd seen a necklace with pendants of a dove and a stone. I tied the message into motherhood, peace, and wisdom. I wrote Quinn a note of gratitude from Cole for being a brave mother and a wise person in making a good choice for his future. Quinn wore this necklace to our first lunch meeting with Cole.

Elle

A little while after meeting Rachel and our new baby (and Dan, the biological dad), Jack and I were sitting in a back room with Trudy, the head nurse of the nursery, who was our absolute savior. She asked if I would be breast-feeding. Wow! I had no idea this was even an option. I said no, and she then taught us how to properly give a bottle to a newborn. Harper's first feeding was magical; she polished off her formula within minutes. In fact, Trudy exclaimed, "Holy crap, she's a few ounces over where she should be; pull back the bottle! I don't want her stomach to explode." Naturally, this put me in a tailspin. That would be just my luck: I harm this beautiful angel during her first feeding. Typical. Then, to add fuel to my already worried state, Jack cried, "Jesus, Elle, pay attention; you're going to kill her." This is not what I needed at that moment. I needed TLC from Jack, not a verbal assault, especially in front of Trudy. This day was making me an emotional basket case on the verge of tears of joy and sorrow, all at the same time.

To my amazement, I already felt an overwhelming bond with this baby, and I had enormous guilt about leaving her in the hospital overnight. I wanted to be there in the middle of the night to hold her and feed her and make certain that she did not feel abandoned. Unfortunately, this hospital, I was told, was not "adoption friendly," so adjoining rooms were not an option. I just had to live with the fact that there would be no "skin-on-skin" time with her for the first few days. (Although those first few days have been more than made up for down the road... if it's truly possible to kiss someone to death, Harper needs to get her last will and testament together ASAP!)

It was a heavenly day; an angel had just been sent to us through another woman's body. Amazing Grace.

"Good (first) night, Harper Appelbaum. Sleep tight, Nugget. You did great on your first day of the rest of your life! I am in love with you completely. Thank you for finding me."

The next morning, we said our final good-byes to Rachel with hugs and kisses. Just before walking out the door, I gave her an envelope containing the following letter and a sentimental gold bangle that I never took off my wrist, a gift from Jack years earlier. Here's the letter:

Dear Rachel,

To even begin to express how incredibly happy Jack and I are is impossible. The past twenty-four hours have included the most joyous moments in our lives and you, Rachel, have made that possible. As I look back at my life, everything now makes sense and falls into perfect place. I know we have expressed it to each other already, but it's worth expressing again that we have truly found each other for a reason. I never really understood before yesterday at 8:28 a.m. what it meant when people say, "It was meant to be." Now, luckily, I do.

Rachel, first and foremost, I want you to know that she will be given the best possible life. She will be loved deeply... these things I promise you. You are so beautiful, Rachel. I know there is nothing in this world that I can give you that can measure up to the gift you have just given us, but

Dear ♡ Child

I want you to have this bangle that Jack gave me at the beginning of our marriage, on my birthday, symbolizing his love for me and Kaki (our dog), who had just survived her first round of cancer. The emerald symbolizes the month of May in which Kaki and I were born... now we get to add this angel you have blessed us with to the list... May 18.

For Always and Ever... Love,

Elle

Chapter ♡ Six
Who's Your Daddy?

Adoption is the ultimate joint venture. And the husbands of Sydney, Elle, Julia, and Ginger took each step with their wives, sometimes leaping ahead, sometimes deferring. They were riding the roller coaster together. The biological fathers were a different story. They might be the missing piece of the puzzle—a dry, cryptic statement of an unknown on an official form. Or they might be dramatic, teary-eyed presences during the birthing process. It was a huge relief was that none of the biological dads challenged the adoption.

In the world of adoption, there are a lot of unknowns, especially when it comes to the biological father. For us, every birth mom lead except one had an unknown or only possible biological dad. Faced with this mystery, you only want to find out who he is in order to have him waive his rights as the dad.

One lead from our adoption agency had an "unknown" biological dad. But when we flew across the country to Philadelphia to meet the birth mom, all she did was talk about the "baby daddy." She joked about his lips, saying, "If my girl comes out with her daddy's lips, I'm pushing her back in." This led her to share that she was having a biracial baby, which was okay by us. But for Phillip, the writing was on the wall that this was not a firm match; as it turned out, they decided to keep the baby with support from both families.

We knew that having an open adoption could mean not knowing the biological dad and having to finalize the adoption without any documented release from him. But we got lucky. Our biological dad was more worried about getting out of paying child support than he was about what would happen to his son. He didn't ask for contact, and we didn't care.

What we did know was that the he was the missing link to Quinn's life and her inability to raise a child. And it was heartwarming to see Quinn acknowledge Phillip as Cole's daddy from the start. We heard the sad "break-up" stories from Quinn and we even met the biological dad's mother and stepsister when they visited at the time of Cole's birth. We planned to ask more during their short visit to say good-bye to Cole, but we didn't have to. As we sat in Quinn's hospital room, the biological dad's mom acknowledged her son was immature and irresponsible, and apologized to Quinn for it.

The only things we'll be able to share with Cole are his biological dad's name, that he was in his eighth year of a Ph.D. program, and that he was six foot, five inches tall, and dark and handsome. His genetic blend of English, Irish, and Spanish was similar to Phillip's. But all that really mattered was that he had enough wisdom to sign over his rights for his son to be adopted.

Cole will look back on a photo of Phillip cutting the cord and handing him to me the minute he was born, and what he will grow to love and respect is the relationship he will have with Phillip as his father. They will have many of the same likes due to living together intimately as father and son. They will build a lifetime of memories as father and son that nothing else can replace. And, if it were to matter to Cole someday, we are prepared to seek and find what we can about his biological father, to give him greater knowledge of his DNA.

I sometimes think how the lack of future relationship with any other father means that Phillip won't need to share Cole; whereas I know the day will come when Cole is acquainted with his birth mom more closely, and I wonder how I'll feel sharing the role of mom. Phillip will always be regarded as the provider and the one who was "there" for Cole when he needed a dad. Phillip not only brought him into the world with the unique experience of cutting the cord. Phillip was there, in the emergency room, while our three-week-old son was tested for what was later determined to be a protein allergy to his formula.

For Phillip, the moment he really bonded with Cole was when his infant son was curled up in a little ball, squeezing his daddy's fingers as tightly as a three-week-old newborn could grip, while enduring a spinal tap. Those two experiences with Cole are enough for us to know that Phillip is his daddy!

Ginger

During our seven years of attempted baby-making, I was so absorbed in my own world that I rarely took time to see our life from Gordon's perspective. It was very clear that, biologically, the challenges rested with me. After one of many semen analyses, a nurse called him a "stud." Still, infertility was our problem.

Early on, my regular Ob-Gyn said, "Just live a regular life for six months and see what happens. Relax. Take a vacation." After six months of targeted baby-making sex without a pregnancy, I was reviewing next steps with my doctor, and mentioned that Gordon and I were enjoying our new hot tub at cocktail hour. He said, "Gordon shouldn't be hot-tubbing if he's trying to get you pregnant."

Thanks, guy! Now you tell me! Of course, it made sense: I wasn't getting pregnant because we had cooked our swimmers. There goes six months lost! So I did more research and laid down the law for Gordon: no bike shorts, no hot tubs, and no pot. Here came the shift—from loving wife and romantic partner to bossy wannabe mommy! But that didn't worry me: I was flying high, convinced that now I'd get pregnant immediately. Ha!

And, by the way, there's nothing sexy about baby-making sex. You're timing when you can, when you can't, and when you have to after a positive ovulation test. Gordon got lots of advice from his friends, too. My favorite was from Jason, father of three: "Point your toes." (Hope you get that.)

As unpleasant as much of the process was (it can't be fun ejaculating into a cup at a doctor's office!), Gordon was very supportive. When we changed strategies and moved to adoption, and once Gordon was committed, he felt and acted with great enthusiasm. I can't say there was an aha moment for him about adoption; it was more about allowing time for the idea to sink in, so he felt more comfortable with it. He needed to agree on his terms without feeling pushed or bullied. Understandable.

Once Gordon was in, he was *all* in. He initiated meetings with counselors. And he helped prepare the house for the dreaded home study. (Did he really need to rush to complete the deck project before the home visit? Probably not: the social worker didn't even look outside. But he did —thanks, honey!) He even hung flyers about our family in Laundromats and coffee shops during a trip to Oregon.

During the process, there were two opportunities for Amber to provide information about the biological father. Our adoption attorney gave us an intake form Amber had completed during her pregnancy and the biological father section listed a first and last name. Later, when our baby, Olivia, was a day old, Amber completed a second form with the local adoption agency and the birth father was listed as "unknown." Gordon immediately called attention to this discrepancy. But the attitude of some of the "professionals" was that we were being unreasonable. The form they were using showed "unknown" and they were running with that story. The feeling we got was that they didn't want to create more stress for everyone, and they justified their inaction by saying it was unlikely the biological father would be found anyway. It was clear there was no relationship between Amber and the biological father, so she may have even gotten the name wrong… why rock the boat?

Gordon would not stand for it. He called out the fact that a full name was given, and insisted that we had an obligation to find this man. The lawyer in Gordon (he's licensed to practice law) knew the biological father had rights. The dad in Gordon knew looking for him was the right thing to do, both for the sake of the child and the biological father. Gordon reminded me of an adoption counselor's advice: *In decision-making, act in the best interest of the child... not the attorney, not the agency, not even the birth family or yourself. Ask yourself what is best for the child.* Without a doubt, the best thing for Olivia was to make an effort to find her biological father.

Melinda, our adoption attorney, supported our decision and found a private investigator to run a search. Unfortunately, we were unable to locate the biological dad. Gordon said, at least he'd be able to tell his daughter some day that we tried to find her biological father. It does seem terribly unfair that he has no knowledge of all that transpired and the incredible impact his "contribution" had on our lives. I wondered what his reaction would be.

Additional details were listed on the intake forms. The biological dad's description: *six feet tall, brown hair, and brown eyes.* His occupation: *has a great job, a professional.* But I find myself wondering if he has fine hair, like Olivia. Does he burn easily, like Olivia? Does he have an underbite, like Olivia? On the form, under the category of, "I am unable to identify the birth father because..." Amber's answer was: *I only knew him for a few hours.*

You have to laugh at nature... we go through years of crap and it takes Amber a couple hours to meet and bed a guy and make a baby! Life is unfair. But then, we knew that!

Elle

Jack's poignant comment to me revealed his feelings about our adoption journey: "I really think it's cool that I'm a part of this process. You and me are having this baby together and it's 50/50. We are equals. It's not the usual: we have sex and then you get to carry, birth, and breast feed the baby, and I'm just hanging out on the sidelines. I really feel involved and a part of this whole process, and I love it."

After each of our half-dozen meetings with possible birth mom matches, Jack stayed breezy. He'd always predict how easy the process was going to be for us, saying, "Who wouldn't want us as adoptive parents for their baby? We are an amazing family unit: you, Boots (that was his pet name for our Rhodesian Ridgeback, Kaki), and me… we're so awesome!"

Looking back, I can see why Jack used humor so often: Emotionally, he couldn't relive all our failed attempts to get pregnant and the two "wild goose chase" biological mother leads. He was unable to "fix" how I was feeling. So he was going to "fix" things the best way he knew how, with humor, confidence, knowledge, and cold hard facts (not emotions) that were black or white (not every color of the rainbow, like my emotions were and still are). This was his way of coping with me and the unknown of what would happen as we tried to create our family.

Once we were selected, an excited yet very cautious Jack pretty much stepped out of the picture and let me lead "the show." Jack did participate in my second phone conversation with Rachel, and it was very awkward for him. He kept looking at me, his piercing blue eyes pleading for me to do all the talking and coddling.

Jack's second meeting with Rachel was at the hospital, a few minutes after Harper was born. Which brings us to Dan—the biological father—the second man of the hour, the other half of the "equation," that made all our dreams come true.

I first "met" Dan on page three of the Birth Mother Medical Background form that Rachel faxed to our agency. I was excited to learn his racial/ethnic heritage was African-American, Italian, and Puerto Rican: an amazingly beautiful mix of genes. *Wow!* I remember thinking. "This baby is going to be absolutely gorgeous." With Rachel being Irish, German, and Cherokee, hot damn, this baby was going to be the Next Top Model. I wanted to meet Dan… I *had* to meet him. My wish came true when Jack and I arranged to phone him thirteen days later. That whole day my stomach was doing flip-flops. I wanted to throw up. I felt like (and I was) getting ready for the next biggest interview of my life.

What really made it excruciating for me was he didn't pick up my first eight calls to his home phone (one call every five minutes). So, once again, there I was, stalking the birth parent on my first meeting with them. Not only did he deserve the call even if he was late for it, but our baby deserved the call. I remember thinking, *I will not leave this chair until I get Dan on the phone.* I will never tell our baby that I did not fight to find out everything I could about Dan, her "(Don't Be) Tardy for the Party" birth father. I dialed his number for the eighth time and, after the tenth ring, a confident and strong "Hello" answered the phone.

Dan gave me some lame-ass excuse to explain why he was forty minutes late for our scheduled call. He continued by stressing to me how much he loved and cared for Rachel and supported her decision to put the baby up for adoption 100 percent.

A few days later, Jack and he had a phone call, and they seemed to really hit it off. Dan was intrigued to learn Jack was an ex-Army Ranger and eagerly shared with Jack that his grandfather served in the military. Clearly Jack and he had a completely different conversation than I'd had with Dan. Boys will be boys! I was so happy we met Dan over the phone before the birth. He told us he would be at the hospital, but not in the delivery room, to comply with Rachel's wishes. Hmmmm... great. Dan seemed to be playing his role with grace and consideration. But when the big day came, his cool veneer fell apart to reveal a lot of raw emotion churning beneath the surface.

Right after Rachel gave birth, Jack and I spent quiet time in her room with newborn Harper and Rachel's parents. Then a nurse poked her head in and told us Dan was on his way to our room. This news definitely brought a shift in the room's positive energy, and Deidre, Rachel's mother, dryly exclaimed, "Oh, great. Everyone, brace yourselves. Here comes drama." And boy, was she right.

Within thirty seconds, Dan burst through the door. He was hyped-up and he smelled of cigarettes and alcohol. I felt the deepest pain for him. His abrupt entrance destroyed the calm in the room, and a heavy tension hung in the air. Not wanting anyone to feel uncomfortable, I greeted him cheerfully and then, without missing a beat, I presented our bundle of joy to him. In a phone conversation we'd had earlier, he'd said he didn't know if he would want to hold the baby. But when I saw him looking so lost and forlorn, I knew the right thing was for him to hold his new baby girl, whom he'd helped bring to this life. Tearfully, he looked at Harper, and choked up upon seeing she was a girl. It was obvious he felt awe that he had a part in creating the beautiful creature he was holding in his arms.

Almost as if on cue, two nurses rushed into the room, one nurse taking the baby to get cleaned up and checked into the nursery, and the other nurse insisting that Jack, Dan, and I come with her. As the nurse ushered us down the hall, she kept ohhing and ahhing over how beautiful Harper was. Not feeling that I could take any credit, I looked over and smiled at Dan who was tearing up. My heart was breaking for him. He was experiencing the loss. The reality that this baby was not going to be a part of his life was sinking in for him.

After what seemed like hours, the nurse and Margaret (Rachel and Dan's social worker) took us all down to see the baby in the nursery. While Margaret distracted Dan, the nurse instructed Jack and me to wash our hands, then gave us wristbands that Rachel had given her for us. These wristbands permitted us to enter the nursery any time to hold, feed, and visit the baby. It was heart-wrenching that Dan *wasn't* given one of these magical wristbands. When he realized that Rachel hadn't given him one, he got really pissed off. The nurse, seeing his anger, frantically whisked us away from him and into the nursery, where up front and center, waiting for us, was our gorgeous angel in her crib. I was so overjoyed at seeing her again after those long forty-five minutes, my eyes resumed devouring her and memorizing her every feature. It was so surreal. Again that feeling of guilt and sadness started to seep in and I turned around, expecting to see Dan on the other side of the glass.

But he was nowhere to be found; he was history. That was the last time I saw him or talked to him. To this day, I think about how intense our morning was together, and then he just disappeared without even a good-bye. I'm sure that was the easiest thing for him to do, and I completely understand why there were no good-byes. For me, truly, "good-bye" is the hardest word to say in the English language.

Julia

"Adopt? I really don't feel like that is what we are supposed to be doing. I want to have *our* children… *our* genetics!"

I walked away despondent. I just didn't understand why Oscar was being so contrary. Didn't he realize how badly I wanted children? Didn't he know how much I didn't want to try IVF again? Adoption was our only option, the way I saw it.

We had struggled with the idea of adoption for years. I'd mention it to Oscar, only to have him tell me his feelings again: he was willing to have children but did not want to adopt.

"What if we tried international adoption?" I'd say. "Or maybe domestic adoption would be better because we could possibly have the child from birth." I suggested anything that might tug a heartstring in Oscar. We attended one foster care conference together. At the end of the first morning, there was not a dry eye in the auditorium—including his. I thought, for sure, the heartbreaking stories of how badly children needed homes and families would change his mind.

After that, Oscar began suggesting we try to become foster parents. He said maybe that would be a way to test the waters as far as adoption. But I didn't want to go through one more heartbreak—this time, raising a child for months, only to have the state come one day and tell me the baby had to go back to the birth parents. No, I wanted to make a lifetime commitment to a baby, not rescue him or her for a few months and then left with an empty nest.

I think it was fear that kept Oscar from saying yes. People tell so many horror stories about adopted children and difficult family situations, stories of rebellious children or hopeless parents. Too often, it's the terrible stories that get told and not the good ones. And I think that's where Oscar was stuck. He was afraid that the horror story would happen to us. He was afraid that someone else's genetics would produce a child who was nothing like either one of us.

I continued to express my desire for adoption. Oscar continued to express his discomfort. But I felt his opposition softening. We talked to work associates about their great experience adopting two children. And we spoke with friends who'd fostered children and loved the experience. There were gaps creeping into Oscar's resistance.

We had dinner with our friends Sydney and Phillip and met their adopted son, Cole. That evening, Oscar saw firsthand how happy they were, and how beautiful the adoptive relationship could be. Sydney and Phillip had brought Cole home from the hospital at birth. The notion of having our child from day one appealed to Oscar. It eased his fear of the hurt and abandonment that are so damaging to children left to bounce around the foster care system or who are neglected in an orphanage for months, if not years. Now, years later, with Benjamin in our lives, we often joke that if anyone is going to screw this child up from the beginning, we want it to be *us*!

Oscar's fears weren't completely laid to rest upon meeting Cole. But they were calmed enough for us to decide to start the adoption process.

There were soon other obstacles. Time—in the form of required parenting classes—and money. Lots of money. Home study fees, background check fees, agency fees, class fees, attorney fees: they all began to add up. Oscar is the frugal one in the family; however, I'd been put in charge of figuring out the total costs of adoption. That was a bad plan, considering the fact that one of Oscar's pet peeves about me is my complete inability to remember numbers or prices. My perception of the cost of adoption and the reality were two different things. This wasn't reassuring to Oscar either.

Then we went to adoption class, a weekend long course required in order to complete our home study. I thought it would be informative, equipping us with the knowledge and tools to parent an adopted child. I was looking forward to it. Oscar, on the other hand, prizes his weekends. It's his time to unwind and play. A beautiful weekend wasted inside a classroom? Not his cup of tea. After sixteen hours of videos, guest speakers, group sessions, and workbooks, Oscar was officially freaked out. If he was wary of adoption before this class, he was terrified after! It was horror story after trauma after heartbreak in the class. I figured they were trying to prepare us for the worst, but Oscar feared every one of those scenarios would happen to us. I was discouraged again. I'd hoped this class would fill us both with joyful anticipation, but it did none of that. However, Oscar was committed—whether he was comfortable with it or not. And we proceeded down the road toward our baby together.

Months went by and the silence from Hope, our adoption facilitator, was frightening. Neither of us was getting younger and my biological clock wasn't just ticking, it had exploded. There was a strange new dynamic between Oscar and me. It was like the huge elephant in the room that no one wanted to talk about. We were going about our lives as if nothing were happening... or going to happen. Vacations, dinner parties, redecorating the house, work: we could talk about everything else. But we couldn't talk about or plan for the fact that we might have a child . . . because it might never happen. Oscar was okay with that. He'd had a family in his previous marriage and three wonderful sons who fulfilled that part of his life.

His sons accepted the idea of having another sibling. Although not excited, they never showed any negativity toward our goal. They knew we were committed to each other and to having a family. Two of his sons had families of their own and his third was busy with his social and professional life, so our child would probably have little impact on their daily lives.

Oscar's commitment was evident, though. The day we found out that Laura had chosen us to be her son's parents, he was ecstatic. We cried happy tears together and he couldn't wait to tell his family. As I called my sister and parents, he called his own parents and then his sons. I could hear the joy in his voice. It meant the world to me. The adoption path held its challenges for Oscar, but he'd taken each one in stride. And now that we knew our son was on the way, I could feel the joy and excitement build in him.

We were a team in our preparations. Oscar strategized our upcoming drive to California with me, and I ran furniture and paint color choices for the nursery by him. When we got the call that Laura was in labor, I packed little Benjamin's bag and we were on the road in thirty minutes. Oscar is a great road-tripper and he sped through the night most of the way there.

Throughout the night, Jonathan, the biological dad, sent Oscar texts and a picture about baby Benjamin's status. Since he was in the NICU, we were eager to get each one. The lone photo showed Benjamin connected to all kinds of wires and tubes. We were both frightened by his appearance, but Jonathan texted Oscar again that, "Benjamin is doing better and he's a fighter… like me." I wondered what it must feel like to be taking pictures of your newborn son and sending them to the man who would be raising him. Through his kindness and fortitude, it was as if Jonathan were giving us glimpses into the personality our son would grow into.

When we arrived at the hospital, we saw Jonathan first in the waiting room, waiting for us to arrive. He stood up and firmly shook Oscar's hand. Again, I wondered about Jonathan's feelings. In a way, it was almost ceremonial. Jonathan was there at the beginning of Benjamin's life, and was now passing on the baton to Oscar to finish the job.

We walked into the NICU together to meet Benjamin for the first time… and Oscar was a daddy again. He never looked back.

Chapter ♡ Seven
Open Door to Open Adoption

Elle, Julia, Ginger, and Sydney all chose open adoption because they felt it was best for the child, particularly as the child's life unfolded. They also loved what openness implied: adoption isn't a dark secret but, rather, a miracle to be celebrated. In reality, their choice meant being open to all possibilities, including unexpected and unwelcome ones. But, despite some disappointment, none of them regret the choice. They remain open to positive changes.

Sydney

When Philip and I considered all our possible adoption choices—international, do-mestic, and all the variations of closed and open—we felt open adoption would be the best way to go. International seemed to be getting more complicated in one country after the next. Since we definitely wanted things to go smoothly and quickly, domestic adoption was for us.

We learned there are three possible levels of contact between biological par-ents and adoptive families: open, semi-open, and closed. The difference between them is how much contact, if any, the adoptive family, and possibly the child, have with the biological parents. Closed adoption was a popular form of adoption in past generations but is now rare. These days, the norm is some contact between bi-ological parents and adoptive families, either before and after the child's birth, only before, or only after. So the most popular options today are semi-open or open.

When Phillip and I chose open adoption, we knew we were adopting more than a baby; we'd be adopting the situation of the birth mom, and each birth moth-er would have her own circumstances and contact wishes. At that early point, we didn't yet know how the biological parents would feel about contact. But we knew how we felt. And we were certain it was in the best interest of the child to have an understanding of where he or she came from, and to have contact with one or both biological parents once the child was ready for it and if desired by all involved. Our expecting mother letter stated this belief on the front cover "openly":

We feel that open adoption is best for a child and look forward to the time when your child is ready to learn and understand more about you and his or her birth story. We will encourage a love and acceptance for you and the choices that you have made and feel that honesty will only strengthen and empower a child's confidence and security.

Julia

Before adopting, I always felt "open" was the way to go. I believed it would be the healthiest option emotionally for everyone involved. The biological parents, the adoptive parents, and the child all have a transparent relationship from the start. There are no secrets, no unanswered questions. It's a win-win. Oscar agreed. We'd both seen enough movies and heard stories of the child who finds out when he's sixteen that he was adopted and the knowledge devastates his life. Open adoption seemed to us like the rational way to avoid catastrophe.

And then we adopted. I soon realized that open adoption was going to be way more complicated than I'd imagined. With open adoption, nothing is cut and dry. What are the rules? What are the expectations? How involved are we in lives of the biological parents, and vice versa? Our son currently has three biological siblings. Will Benjamin ever have contact with them? Will he want to? Will they want to meet him? To me, "open" began to feel more like "open-ended."

Ginger

We were "open" to open, especially after hearing about positive experiences between biological families and adoptive families who went this route. Do they even *do* closed adoptions anymore? In our research, open was definitely promoted as most popular and more beneficial to all parties. Perhaps this was due to our touchy-feely geography—we live in northern California—but it really didn't seem like closed was even an option. I did wonder what research had been done to support the commonly held belief that open is better for the child. If we lived in a laboratory, it would be interesting to see the outcome for a child in an open adoption and, in a parallel universe, to see the same child grow up in a closed adoption.

During our research, I conducted my own "study." In a unique twist of fate, two of my best friends, Meg and Sophie, were adopted. I met them in college, but they'd been close to each other since grade school, perhaps bonding over the shared experience of being adopted. They were born in a generation when closed adoption was the norm. And each had a completely different outlook on biological families.

Meg had a real yearning to have questions answered, to meet her biological mother and to learn about her roots. When asked if she is Swedish—a natural question, since she is blonde with blue eyes—she answers yes, because it's easier. Yet her stunning blue eyes and tall frame set her apart from the rest of her adoptive family. She longs to see a biological relation who looks like her. Meg hasn't taken action because she knows it would upset her mom. Knowing Meg's feelings, I promised myself that if I was lucky enough to adopt, I would be supportive of such a request from my child.

Sophie's mom is the polar opposite, actually encouraging her daughter's interest in her biological parents. To Sophie's mom, there was no competition and no jealousy. But Sophie doesn't want to know. She has told me this is a gap she doesn't need to fill, that she is afraid of what she might find. Instead, she has created an image in her mind of her biological parents that she's comfortable with. Why risk being disappointed if reality falls short of her hopes?

Elle

From the beginning of the adoption process, I was definitely wary of open adoption. I felt this way because I didn't know exactly what an open adoption entailed, coupled with the fact that I'd never met anybody involved in an open adoption who could "sell" me on this concept. So an open adoption scenario just seemed so foreign to me. How does one go about figuring out how and when the biological parent(s) and the adoptive parent(s) engage with each other "x" amount of times a year? And when they're together, how do those dynamics work for them and the child? I mean, heck, Jack and I have our own family dramatics to deal with "x" amount of times a year. So now, we were going to throw *more* families into our Chex Mix of a family? The thought of trying to appease one more person during the holidays, or the birth mom nagging me to cut the baby's hair, or her giving me parenting advice, had me in hives.

But I came to learn through the numerous Q & A sessions we had attended, that open adoption is strongly encouraged today. The traditional adoption script read, "You adopt your child, and his or her adoption is kept a big secret until some family member spills the beans after too many drinks at a family gathering, or you adopt your child and that fact is under wraps until his or her eighteenth birthday, and possibly at that time, you have 'the Talk' and offer some of the bio-parents' info"—this was a scenario of the past. In fact, I was astonished to learn that twenty years ago, one percent of all domestic adoptions were open adoptions while, in 2012, 60 to 70 percent of all domestic adoptions are open. Damn, I'd say that's quite a shift for only two decades!

But enough with statistics. The real skinny on how I felt about open adoption came to a head when I was filling out the adoption forms and one of them asked about this very question. After much deliberating and probably being completely desperate to bring a baby into our lives, I checked the box that said "open" (meaning that I was open to a closed *or* open adoption, whichever scenario the biological mother wanted). I remember feeling a sense of triumph coupled with relief when I checked that box because, internally, I'd been struggling with this question throughout the adoption process. I finally felt at peace, truly open and ready for whichever scenario came our way.

Open adoption is a potential. It comes with no guarantees. Although all four women went into it with open hearts, things didn't always work out as planned. They found creative ways to keep the birth mom in the loop. If she didn't want to, they felt good knowing that if, someday in the future, their children wanted to know their biological parents, it would be easier for them to connect than ever before in history because they chose open adoption.

Sydney

Our biological mother's circumstances: she was a nineteen-year-old who strayed from her family after high school seeking love and companionship. Quinn ended up meeting a thirty-nine-year-old guy online and, after very few weeks together, she got pregnant. She hoped to stay with him and start a family at a young and naïve age, only to have her heart broken when she was eight-and-a-half months pregnant. Quinn quickly ran back home to safety, and was encouraged to make the brave and wise choice of placing her child for adoption.

Happily, Quinn also wanted an open situation. From the very first lunch meeting with her and nearly to the end of the paper signing, open adoption felt like the one known among many unknowns. Little did we know then that our open adoption contact agreement to have twice-a-year visits would end up being far fewer over the years.

However, Phillip and I remain glad we chose the open adoption route. We know things can change with our birth mom. Open adoption leaves the door open.

Julia

Oscar and I decided after Benjamin was born that we would not have official "rules" or a contract regarding how much contact we'd have with his biological parents. I assured Laura we'd send her occasional photos through a Facebook page made specifically for Benjamin. I placed strict privacy settings on the page, ensuring that Laura and Jonathan (Benjamin's biological dad) were the only two people privileged to view his updates. This, it seemed to me, would be a good way to communicate. And, so far, it's been a great way to share the joy that is Benjamin's life. His smile is infectious, and I love being able to reassure Laura through pictures that the choice she made to place him with us was for the best. I post pictures of him playing, pictures of him dressed up for Halloween, and little comments about how he's doing, what he's learning, and how much he's growing. Laura and Jonathan can see that he's happy, healthy, and experiencing things with us as a family. Often, Laura will repost pictures of Benjamin on her page with a comment about "my son." At first, I was uncomfortable with her sharing pictures that were meant only for her. But over time, I've come to believe it's not only her way of showing others that she made a good decision, but a method of healing her own heart.

Our expectations aren't grand concerning the openness of our adoption. We are committed to making an annual visit to California; however, we know we can't control what will happen in Laura's and Jonathan's lives. They may move, or decide they don't want to see us. The certainty of uncertainty comes with the territory of open adoption. But I know it's the best of all possible options for our family.

Ginger

Early on with Amber, we knew there was little chance of an ongoing relationship. Before I had even met Amber, our adoption attorney, Melinda, explained that Amber had placed a boy with a family eighteen months earlier, and that there had been no ongoing contact. Would this time be different? The fact that Amber didn't follow through with plans to meet for lunch during our stay in Ohio led us to believe history would repeat itself.

Still, we sent letters with photos to Amber through Melinda. The fact that we couldn't send them directly to Amber demonstrates the various degrees of "open." Basically, all we had was Amber's first and last name. While she seemed to move around a lot, Melinda always had her current contact information, so she was the go-between.

We received no response from Amber to our letters and the enclosed photos of Olivia changing from infant to baby to toddler. Too painful for her? Did she not want to revisit and reopen the sadness of giving up a baby? I try not to imagine it was a general lack of interest. Whatever the reason, although we remain open to "open," we have no contact with Amber. Perhaps that will change in the future.

I feel lucky that at least *I* had some time with her, so I can tell Olivia about meeting her biological mother. And I cherish the photos of the three of us together, taken when Olivia was one day old. Occasionally, when retelling Olivia her birth story, I show her the photos, so she feels some connection. If Olivia decides she's interested in finding her biological mother one day, I am committed to helping her make the connection.

These days, with donor eggs becoming more common, there are more opportunities for an open dialog with children. My son, Ethan, was conceived through the miracle of a donor egg, but he has a genetic link to my husband. *A family is more than biology.* Still, it is nice to have a genetic connection as well, and to see glimpses of Gordon in Ethan. I tell my kids that each of them is one of a kind, a special mix.

I read an article recently about a woman who spent years trying to get pregnant through IVF. She insisted on having a biological link to her child, so adoption was out of the question. Hey, good for her, but I consider that to be a very limited mindset. Why does a biological link have such critical importance? What makes shared DNA so significant? Consider this: you love your husband (or partner) and there is no biological connection. And don't forget to weigh the fact that a woman might spend boatloads of time and money holding onto the goal of a genetic link and *still* end up childless. For women under thirty-five, the success rate for IVF averages 60 percent. While adoption takes some patience, the success rate is 100 percent.

Elle

As it turned out, Rachel (Harper's birth mom) expressed the following in the Birthmother Medical Background form she completed for my adoption agency:

"I wish for this child to be raised in a warm and nurturing environment. As an adopted child myself, I understand the questions that may arise as he or she grows into a young man or woman. I wish to continue providing my contact information if this baby were to have questions for or want to meet me in the future."

After reading this request, I can honestly say I was relieved. I now felt willing to bring more family into the mix if the biological parent(s) wanted this for themselves and the baby, although I still wasn't going to willingly bring this "mix" into play myself. With that said, I felt then as I do now: Harper's adoption and her biological parents are not something to be brushed under the rug. It is something that should be talked about with family and friends (and, of course, Harper). In fact, Harper's birth parents have been and will continue to be talked about and respected because of their courageous and selfless decision to give Harper the best life they saw possible. They saw her having that life in our care… what a humbling, yet mind-blowing honor for them to place her with us.

Ultimately, if it were not for them and the love and compassion they had for each other's futures and the future of the baby they had created, Harper wouldn't be in our lives. Knowing these intricate pieces of the puzzle makes Harper even more precious to me. I continually ask myself, how did I get so lucky to have found this perfect little life who has brought so much happiness into my life? Not a day goes by that I do not look at her and think about all the what-ifs and all the different paths that were taken—some with intent and some without—that led me to her. The remarkable journey that brought us together is definitely something that has been and will continue to be shared and talked about and celebrated. Harper's unique story of how she came to be and how she came into our lives is beyond special and something that I want her to be proud of always.

In the future, if Harper wants to contact Rachel or Dan, I will completely support her decision. I will do anything and everything to help her navigate a path to these pivotal people who brought her into our lives. As I see it, Rachel and Dan have given us the most amazing gift in the world. So why would I stand in the way of their chance to meet and see this beauty they created?

So that Rachel and Dan can understand my feelings, I've written this message for them. I hope that someday, somehow, each of them reads it…

Rachel and Dan,

Words cannot even begin to express the infinite gratitude I have for you both. You two without a doubt have made possible the greatest gift I have received and will ever receive from anyone ever, while I am alive on this earth. The sentiment of 'thank you' almost seems insulting because I want to express something so much deeper than that to you two, but it is simply impossible for me to put into words.

Rachel, please know I think of you every time I soak in her perfectly arched eyebrows that frame her insanely expressive big brown eyes and her plump pink earlobes that are meant to be bitten and her lipstick-stained, heart-shaped pouty lips that I kiss way too much.

Dear ♡ Child

Dan, please know I think of you every time I touch her beautiful cocoa skin and kiss her prominent button of a nose and brush her thick silky chocolate hair with just the perfect amount of wave.

Thank you for making these moments possible. She is absolutely beautiful inside and out… it is impossible not to just devour her (even with her frequent meltdowns of late). Sometimes I kiss this beautiful angel so hard that she gets mad at me. (Sorry, Baby. I just can't help myself!) It's impossible to contain my love and affection for this perfect little life that you two have made possible.

For Always and Ever, I am yours Forever,

Elle

Chapter ♡ Eight
Baby Bond

Though they had thought about and planned endlessly for this moment, it felt very sudden. Each woman went from the limbo of the hospital to holding a warm, sleeping baby in her arms. They were mothers of newborns! Suddenly, Elle, Sydney, Julia, and Ginger were consumed with the practicalities—what to buy, how to diaper, how to cope with the daytime sleepiness. Each day brought small joys. They just kept coming. After so many years of waiting and longing, it had happened. Their lives have opened to include another. And each woman realized it was a rare case of the reality being even better—oh, infinitely better—than the dream.

The morning of the "baby pickup" I was super-excited. During the forty-five-minute drive back to the hotel with our baby, I was *so* the "backseat" driver to Jack... in my own head. I suddenly realized why people put that stupid "Baby on Board" sticker on their minivans. (And, no, I do not have one of those stickers, and I do not drive a mini-van.) When we got to the hotel, my dad and my brother and a few of the valet employees and bellhops were standing curbside like hungry paparazzi—obviously my dad had told them a "special" guest was about to check in. Later, my dad and brother left the hotel misty-eyed, yet with big smiles on their faces. Harper was here!

I comically refer to the first night the baby was in our care at the New Jersey hotel as "fright night." At bedtime, I set up the baby between us in a little "bed" that was a ramped contraption about the size of a cookie sheet with padded sides. (By the way, it's been since deemed unsafe and recalled, so I don't feel like such a freak now for being a hypochondriac all night with her Oreo-ed between us.)

Needless to say, I didn't sleep a wink. I was convinced either Jack or I would fall asleep, roll over on top of her and kill her. It was the longest night of non-sleep I've ever had. I actually wanted morning to come as quickly as possible because, in daylight, I felt completely in control.

Sleep, my favorite pastime, had suddenly become my worst enemy. A dozen times in the middle of the night, I listened intently for Harper's breath, then panicked and flashed the light from my cell phone on her face to make sure she was still breathing. As expected, this little and helpless golden nugget was up every two to three hours around the clock. Her stomach-churning cries sent me to the hotel bathroom where I "scrubbed in" like a surgeon about to operate, and made up her bottle consisting of Enfamil and Evian. (Yep, nothing but the best for my little nugget!) After she downed her few ounces of formula, I burped her, changed her, and put her back in the Oreo position between Jack and me, then lay awake waiting for her next feeding, convinced that if I fell asleep, I'd kill her with one body shift. This "fright night" routine lasted our entire stay at the Westin.

The next day, we made our first family outing to Target. To make sure I was getting the right cool stuff, I perked up my ears when I was around the newborn gear, and listened and watched the other moms or soon-to-be moms. The moms already with a child got double bonus points, and I mirrored their every product choice, literally throwing the same stuff in my basket. Thankfully, Harper slept through her first retail experience, so it was an enjoyable shopping trip for all.

After a few days, Jack started taking the train into Manhattan to work, so I got to have her all to myself during the day. This alone time with her was so precious, I just held her and kissed her and drank her up. Yummy. Every morning, I'd stroll Harper through the lobby and say my morning "hellos" to the hotel staff who, by this point, had gotten to know us. Then I'd make my way to the water, where I'd point her stroller toward Manhattan and we'd share the view, while I thought about some of the crazy adventures I'd had there in my twenties. It was beyond perfect and oh-so-comforting that I got to welcome and begin to know my new nugget against the backdrop of my favorite place in the whole world, NYC.

Toward the end of our second week in Jersey, Jack and I were asked to come to HAPS (Homestudies and Adoption Placement Services) to pick up the documents that Rachel and Dan had signed, putting Harper in our temporary legal custody, as well a form that would let us travel with Harper if airport security asked for her ID on our way home to San Francisco.

It was already Thursday and we were a little freaked out because, with the Memorial Day holiday weekend coming up, the Westin as well as all the surrounding hotels were booked solid. We knew that if we didn't get clearance to leave the state by Friday, we'd be stranded in New Jersey——hotel-less—until at least Tuesday after the holiday, as government offices would obviously be closed.

After much reflection, Jack and I made the hard decision to take the risk and fly illegally back home with the baby the next day, Friday. We reasoned that, number one, we already had the legal documentation Rachel and Dan had signed off on (granting us *temporary* custody of the baby until our court hearing in six months), so we were *not* babynapping; and, number two, all we were waiting for was a phone call from HAPS that a copy of the forms already in our possession had made it to California and been verbally "approved" by some pencil-pusher in some random cubical at the State Capitol in Sacramento; what's more, the phone call we'd be receiving on my cell phone could be picked up equally well in New Jersey or California. No one would know we weren't physically in New Jersey—except, of course, our dog Kaki, who was missing us big time. We also reasoned that if some unforeseen circumstance went down and we had to be in New Jersey, we'd simply hop a flight right back to the East Coast. After our final round of room service that Friday morning, we bid farewell to the Westin.

Then, on the way to the airport, the most amazing thing happened… we got *the* call that we could go home. So, thankfully, no laws ended up being "bent." Whew, we'd dodged yet another bullet. California, here we come!

As you can well imagine, I was a complete nervous wreck worrying about all the germs that awaited us at the airport and on the airplane that would bring us back to our beloved city by the bay. Because I didn't want anyone to breathe on her or even touch her, when we got to the ticket counter, I strapped Harper onto Jack in the Baby Bjorn and draped a lightweight blanket over her head so she'd be completely covered from head to toe.

After making our way with all the new baby crap that we had to carry through security, Jack and I stopped at a wine bar next to our gate and celebrated our success in getting through the airport seamlessly with baby in tow and the three of us leaving town in a legal fashion. We did it! We pulled it off!!! We were finally bringing our baby girl home to meet her canine big sister, Kaki.

Sydney

Nothing can prepare you for the moment when the process of adoption is almost complete, but it doesn't yet feel quite real. I think back on the day we took Cole home from the hospital and often reminisce with Phillip about our two "forever" memories of that day. We remember them as if they happened yesterday.

I was confident my home was prepared, and felt comfortable during the three-day transition in the hospital, sharing bedsides with Quinn and taking turns passing Cole among all the many visitors. But the day we actually walked out the door and put Cole and his car seat into our car brought with it an overwhelming sense of guilt that clouded the joy I was feeling. I had to keep reassuring myself that Quinn would get over the loss and move on with her life, and that our open adoption was structured so she'd feel the least loss possible. Seeing each other twice a year would certainly reassure us both of our roles and responsibility in Cole's life. At least I hoped it would.

After saying our tearful "See you in a few months" to Quinn, Phillip and I had a two-hour drive home in separate cars. We had no idea what Cole's feeding schedule would be like any more than what it would feel like to have a "baby on board." Phillip graciously let me be the driver of the "baby on board" car, and because of the Revere mirror installed behind Cole's backward-facing car seat, Phillip didn't worry about how many times I'd feel the urge to turn and look at my son. As I drove ultra-cautiously, I reflected on that first drive to meet the birth mom, remembering how I'd peeked at myself dozens of times in the rearview mirror to reassure myself she'd approve of me. Then I needed to reassure myself I would be a capable parent. Before touching the accelerator, I double-checked all my driver safety needs, like the hands-free phone setup. Of course, I was dying to call everyone and to also stay in touch with Phillip in the car ahead.

The first call I made, barely out of the hotel parking garage, was to my dear friend Samantha, a friend who had supported me through all my highs and lows with infertility, trying with a surrogate, and meeting birth moms. I was so lucky she was willing to drop everything and listen to me cry. My first words to her that day were, "I feel like I just stole someone's baby." Samantha reassured me that our son would feel like ours once we got home, and even got me laughing.

Meanwhile, I felt such anxiety about keeping Cole happy. I had Phillip on standby to pull over the minute Cole made a sound so we could check on him and feed or change him. Needless to say, we never had to pull over; Cole was a champ all the way home. Although, for our own sakes, we still made a few stops to ease our minds that our baby was still breathing. One errand was to buy Cole a swing. Why I felt getting a swing for Cole was so important on the very first day he was home with us is still beyond me. He did enjoy the swing, although he isn't really into swings to this day!

Two funny things happened when we stopped for lunch and Babies R Us. The lunch stop was where it really hit me: I went into the bathroom, looked in the mirror barefaced and wearing a hospital ID band, and decided that I looked pretty good for having a newborn. The second stop was at Babies R Us, where we were asked by a customer also looking at swings for a baby shower gift, "How old does a baby need to be to go into a swing?" I stopped to think, and Phillip proudly said, "Our baby is three days old and we're putting him in it when we get home." She looked me up and down and said, "Did you just leave the hospital?" "Yes," I quickly replied, with no time to explain, and she exclaimed, "You are a rock star!" Phillip smiled at me, murmuring, "Just go with it!" It was the first moment, on day three, when I knew I was not only a mom, but a mother with an adoption story. And that I wasn't ready to tell it.

When we got home, I longed to put Cole in a place where I could just sit and stare at him. It was a moment that would confirm he was 100 percent ours. A moment that would become forever in our three lives. Just as I was settling down with him on the couch, our adoption attorney called. I couldn't help smiling with the expectation that she was calling to tell me yet more protocols—and she was. Her first words were, "Make sure you call your birth mom and tell her you and baby have arrived home safely." She continued, "Oh, and don't forget to ask how she is doing, and to confirm your next visit… And remember, you are technically just babysitting until she signs the final release."

Ugh. Not the worry again. The bliss I had been feeling from being home with our son turned to a sick feeling. After three days of doing "the dance" in the hospital, after our painfully tear-jerking, "Good-bye; see you in a few months," and after the long journey home, I had to venture back down the roads of unknowns?

I instantly called Hope, Quinn's adoption facilitator, to ask if we had all the consent forms signed. Honestly, it was a bit puzzling that I wasn't given this information upon leaving the hospital. Calling Hope was like taking a magic pill of relief. Her very straightforward and supportive words to me were, "Girlfriend, that baby is all yours. Now turn off your phone and don't have an overload of visitors. And enjoy being a mom."

And so I did.

Julia

The day we were allowed to bring Benjamin home from the hospital in California couldn't have come soon enough. It finally arrived when he was seven days old. Because Oscar was still in Colorado taking care of business, his sister came with me to the hospital to bring Benjamin home to Oscar's parents' home. I was grateful for the help—she was a nurse—and I felt confident knowing I had "backup" if things got tough.

It was a bright and clear day, after many days of rain. The air was crisp, but the sun was warming. We brought Benjamin's car seat into the nursery, and when we buckled him in, his tiny body almost disappeared under all the straps. I drove home to my in-laws as if I had a stack of priceless crystal champagne flutes in the back seat. I took each corner incredibly slowly so as not to break my precious cargo.

The first days out of the hospital were a little difficult, but mostly wonderful. I tried to maintain a normal life as much as I could, going on brief walks with Benjamin wrapped tightly to my chest, venturing out to Target, and even taking a conference call with a client who had no idea I was out of town, let alone had just "had" a baby! I would lie in bed for hours on end watching my son sleep next to me. I must have taken five hundred photos to send to Oscar. My joy at being a mother overshadowed my weariness from lack of sleep. But the fact was I was still adjusting to waking every three hours at night and to caring for Benjamin pretty much by myself. It was a lot of change, very fast! In a way, it was nice to not have anything else to do except be with my son. I didn't have a house to clean or meals to prepare: Oscar's parents took good care of us. It gave me time to settle in to being a mother and to get to know my boy all by myself.

After Oscar returned to California, he, Benjamin, and I had lunch with Laura and Jonathan, the biological parents. I was afraid it would be hard to say good-bye, but our eagerness to get home and Laura's positive attitude made it easy. Laura was wearing the necklace I'd given her in the hospital the week before. It was as if she had given us this great gift, and in return, by wearing the necklace, she acknowledged that she was ready to move on. It was a new beginning for us both.

Even now, with Benjamin with us, our lives were still in limbo. All I wanted was to bring our baby home to Colorado and introduce him to our family. But the law prevented us from doing that just yet: we still awaited the State of California's approval to take Benjamin home to Colorado.

So, while waiting, Oscar and I decided to head to Lake Tahoe and stay with our good friends Sydney, Phillip, and their eighteen-month-old adopted son, Cole, at their beautiful lake home. Not only was it *right* on the state line, so we'd have a head start on the anxiously awaited trip home, but it also gave us a chance to introduce Phillip and Sydney to our sweet boy. We packed up our family and hit the road,

Tahoe-bound!

The call came late that afternoon, before we even arrived at their home. Our adoption agency informed us the paperwork had gone through. We could leave the state with our son! Finally, our life as a family could begin.

I felt a sense of freedom as we left the Sacramento area. Tears filled my eyes as a familiar song came on the car radio: *"Suddenly, the world seems such a perfect place/ suddenly, it moves with such a perfect grace/ suddenly, my life doesn't seem such a waste/ it all revolves around you now."* This was the song Oscar sang to me when we were dating, and that I sang back to him. It was our love song, yet "suddenly," we'd become three, and now it was a love song to our child, too! Joy welled up in my heart and I praised God that we were finally here—at this point in my life that I'd spent years praying for. At the top of our lungs and crying, we sang together to Benjamin, *"Come what may, come what may/ I will love you until my dying day."*

At Phillip and Sydney's home, it felt like our journey had come full circle— from the time we met them and discovered each others' struggles with infertility, to their adoption journey, to the chance encounter on the freeway two weeks earlier, to that meeting at their house. We both had families now and could celebrate together. It was perfect—a beautiful beginning to the story of our family, intertwined with two of the people who knew it best.

We left for Colorado on a snowy morning two days later. The drive should've taken two days, but Benjamin was such a champ, and slept the entire time, only awakening for bottles and diaper changes. So Oscar put pedal to the metal through the desert of Nevada and we made it home in one day. The next days and weeks were a blur of sleeplessness, family and friend visits, and utter joy. Our friends and families all knew what a long and often painful journey this had been for Oscar and me. And now our baby was home! My long-awaited life as a mom had begun.

Ginger

After four days in the hospital with Baby, my husband Gordon arrived. He'd been at home preparing to come to Ohio, arranging childcare with relatives for our son Ethan, and pulling baby goods out of storage. I'd had a vision of Gordon's first meeting with Baby—a quiet, bonding experience—but, in reality, their first time together was shared with doctors and social workers.

In order to leave the hospital, Amber, the biological mother, had to sign a relinquishment. This was a stressful process for us; I can only imagine what it must have felt like for her. She did sign. And once the paperwork was completed, we were free to leave the hospital with Baby, but not the state. We had to stay in Ohio until the transfer to California was completed by the courts.

After we were released from the hospital, we celebrated our freedom with a mad dash to Babies R Us. Ethan, was already three-and-a-half, and I discovered I'd already forgotten all the tools and accessories needed for a baby! By the time we found the store, we had just thirty minutes before closing time. I laughed to myself. I'd spent nine months preparing for Ethan's arrival: picking out the right colors, testing softness of sheets and blankets (well-meaning friends instructed me to "Wash everything beforehand in Dreft!"), and analyzing every detail down to the scented paper that lined his dresser. For Baby, I had half an hour to round up the bare necessities.

Although our short-term residency in Ohio was frustrating, this mini-vacation created a bubble for Gordon, Baby, and me, in which we could spend our days nesting. We had no friends or family to visit and no interruptions from work. We were sequestered from the world. We slept and ate a lot. We played with Baby. We felt overwhelmed, but laughed our way through the rough spots. I kept singing in my head, *I got what I wanted, I got what I wanted*, feeling like a spoiled child.

Looking back, it was the perfect welcome for Baby. This sweet pause in time allowed for transition, an introduction into our family. It sounds so cliché, but this was prime bonding time with our new daughter.

One part of our adventure was deciding on a name for Baby. Because she was born in Ohio, for her first week of life, we playfully called her "Buckeye" after the Ohio State University mascot. Our attorney was not amused. She told us, "As your legal counsel, I strongly advise you to change that name in the immediate future."

Actually, I'd already named my daughter a long time ago. While trying to conceive, I had often envisioned a baby—a soul, really—floating around the universe and trying to find its way to me. I had fervently hoped this baby was a girl, and I planned on naming her Olivia. During an IVF cycle, I even went to a perfume-making studio and created a custom scent with that name. Like I said, *Olivia was always out there, finding her way to me.* On day seven, we called the family to announce Olivia's arrival!

The beautiful thing was we were able to transition in phases. The next phase was bringing Olivia home to California. I couldn't wait to introduce big brother Ethan to his new sister. We'd been very cautious about building expectations of adding a sibling in case we weren't successful. I didn't want Ethan to get caught up in an emotional roller coaster. And, of course, up to that point, Ethan was the center of our universe. Now, this three-year-old's world was about to be rocked.

Finally, after eleven days, we got the call that the courts had cleared the paperwork and we were free to bring Olivia home!

Sydney, Ginger, Elle, and Julia were fascinated by detailed discussions of baby poop. They saw sides of their husbands they'd never known existed. They discovered they loved all the ordinary duties of being a mom. None of the women really had a plan for telling people about the adoption, and they found that sometimes it felt right to just pop out with it. They took nothing for granted; each woman had waited too long for it all. Overnight, their lives had changed in dozens of big and small ways, and they wondered whether their happiness would just keep increasing.

Elle

One of the most amazing sights I've ever seen happened the first Saturday morning we were all finally back home. I walked out of my closet and saw our sweet dog and "firstborn," Kaki, in her usual position on our bed, curiously sniffing and then laying alongside an eyes-wide-open Harper. Thankfully, I was able to capture on my iPhone that very first tender and curious moment between Kaki and her new baby sister.

Other out-of-the-norm "firsts" or things I wasn't prepared for those first few weeks back home included:

1. The wierdest sensation of not going to work for the first time literally since middle school, as officially I was out of the "retail biz" and into the "mom biz."
2. UPS and FedEx showing up daily with gifts galore from people I didn't know.
3. Strangers coming up to me in public and commenting on how fabulous I looked after "giving birth," and asking me to share my "secret."
4. Driving the speed limit at all times when baby was on board.
5. Going from pre-baby eating *out* every night after work at restaurants, belly up to the bar, to post-baby eating *in* every night with a baby sleeping on my belly and no bar in sight.
6. Getting "dressed" for my day now meant some sort of Spandex pull-on yoga pants and hoody and no shower. I suddenly "got it" and realized what all these moms were talking about when they'd complain about not having time to shower in the morning.
7. Surfing Diapers.com on a daily basis and doing the laundry and dishes on an hourly basis.
8. Hiking (and stroller-pushing) replacing my usual hard-core running and gym workouts. I'd hike with the baby strapped onto me in the Baby Bjorn because I didn't want her exposed to all the germs that awaited her and ultimately me in the daycare at my gym. Yep, I'd become a germ-o-phobe overnight.
9. A "good night's sleep" now defined as the baby being up every three hours instead of every two.
10. Grabbing coffee with a new mom and finding ourselves comparing and contrasting at great length and with precise detail how my baby's poop and vomit differs from her baby's poop and vomit.

Looking back, it was so crazy how everything changed for me, Jack, and Kaki in just a few weeks. Our empty nest was all of a sudden full and feathered. This "suddenness" that adoption can bring had been explained many times to me by our social workers but it didn't really sink in emotionally until I was experiencing it. So, when you least expect it, expect it.

Sydney

That first afternoon home with our little boy, Phillip busied himself putting the baby swing together and laughing at my inexplicably urgent wish to put Cole in it. Putting toys together and being a dad was a huge desire for Phillip, and he relished the task. He even wanted to change Cole's first diaper!

The next day, Phillip was off to work at seven a.m. after a sleepless night broken up by feedings. But as new parents, it didn't matter. It was all blissful! I was so full of energy I decided to take Cole for a walk in his new stroller, to introduce him to his new town.

The first time I told someone that Cole was adopted was at our neighborhood Starbucks, where everyone knows your name and story. As they took my order and smiled at seeing me with a newborn, I joyfully blurted out, "We adopted!" It was a statement I was going to have to get used to, one I looked forward to Cole learning to say with good feelings.

Every time I tell a story about our open adoption, it opens a new conversation with others. The best thing about open adoption is, finally, having it not be a mystery, with our story just as special as the next. When I reflect on no longer living the dream, but loving the reality, I still find myself thinking of Quinn, wondering what her growth and sense of loss were during the same period that was so miraculous for Phillip and me. During those first days, I comforted myself with the thought that we'd see her in a few months.

Our first three weeks brought us a lot of joy, but even more worry. Our infant went from eating fine in weeks two and the start of three, to being suddenly hit by extreme vomiting during week three, landing us in the ER with no understanding of what was happening to our little boy. This was another point when the lack of mystery with open adoption was reassuring. We called Quinn the minute we were asked genetic questions, and her answers gave the medical staff and us the calming knowledge that there were no genetic issues.

After a week, we learned Cole had a protein allergy and would have to go on specially ordered formula. Not only was our formula three times the cost of regular formula, it was not covered under insurance as a prescription, and we had to order it online, a case at a time. This was just more confirmation of the rightness of this placement: Cole was in a home that could handle such expenses. And the expenses didn't stop there. When Cole was six weeks old, he needed two medical procedures. Going through those experiences with him gave Phillip and me an even deeper sense of our role as parents than if Cole carried our own DNA. We made sure to give Quinn updates, but I sometimes doubted that it was the right thing to do. I worried it suggested that we accepted her as a co-parent.

At two years, we've finally reached a place of contentment concerning our child's birth mom. It consists of very few visits but constant thought. Recently, Quinn sent me an email that gave me a sense of distance and closure. It was something that would serve as the letter she'd said she wanted to write, something I can share with Cole in the years ahead as we help our son understand his adoption.

Here's the email I received from Quinn:

Sydney,

I woke up to this, and I thought I would share it with you, someday share this with Cole.

For My Child

I remember my pregnancy with you

I fell in love with your every move, and with the sound of your beating heart.

I held your precious body in my arms for the first time and took in your sweet, angelic presence.

Nothing could prepare me for what would lie ahead.

Nothing could prevent my heart from breaking, but it had to be done.

Dear ♡ Child

I tried to be strong, but my strength failed me.

I never knew it would be so difficult to write my own name.

I cried, and was grateful for all the precious memories you've given me.

It was a new beginning for you.

The healing was beginning for me.

Time went forward, I learned and grew as I slowly let go of you.

My heart was healed, my life was blessed, and my prayers were answered.

Still, there are days when I cry.

I will never stop thinking about you.

Still I wonder about the person you are now, and the person you've yet to become.

I pray that you will always know of the love I have for you.

It's only through the grace of God that you were mine for a time.

He gave you to me; I lovingly obeyed his plans for you.

Julia

Oscar was a huge help from the beginning. His willingness to take late-night duties gave me the chance to catch up on sleep. He changed diapers, fed bottles, and held Benjamin without a single complaint. I honestly think he enjoyed it! It was an experience that he'd forgotten—or maybe never got—with his older sons. Or maybe he had more time to enjoy the experience than back then. In any case, I think the time he and Benjamin spent together those first weeks and months created a special bond that is evident now.

Despite Oscar's willingness, I wanted to do most of the work myself. I adored holding Benjamin. I didn't mind changing his diapers or giving him late-night feedings. This had been the desire of my heart for so long and, finally, I was getting to enjoy it. It all came really naturally to me and, luckily, Benjamin was an easy baby from the beginning. He only cried when something was really wrong. He ate well, slept often, and was always easy to put to bed. He was quiet and a dream to take out in public. I loved taking him out and showing him off; I beamed with pride as a mother!

Unfortunately, the joy of those first months was short-lived. When Benjamin was two months old, I found out I needed to have an immediate hysterectomy. Unaware of how complicated the surgery and recovery would be, we proceeded. Thankfully, my parents stayed with us for several weeks to care for Benjamin while I convalesced. It was often hard to see him play and hear his cries from the other room and know that I shouldn't, and couldn't, pick him up: doctor's orders. My parents were an unbelievable blessing at that time. Their help in caring for Benjamin let Oscar continue working and gave me time to heal.

I'm sure that during that time, my mom and dad fell head over heels in love with our son, even though they loved him from the start. My dad often remarks to me, "Can you believe you asked me years ago if I would love an adopted child the same as a biological child?" (Honestly, I can't even believe I asked him!)

My family was perhaps Benjamin's biggest fans. I'm pretty sure his sweet face won them over the very first day they saw him, but their love for our little guy still grows. My sister and her kids are crazy about him. Benjamin's cousins ask regularly when he's going to be big enough to play with them. Even though the answer is always "not yet," they love to hold and cuddle him anyway.

The reality of having a family still surprises me on occasion. It's truly better than I could have imagined. I am in love. God promised a family to me years ago. After the heartbreak of miscarriage and the trauma of personal illness, I was broken. But I held on to His promise, and now I get to hold my son. Every day. It's a privilege that I try to never take for granted.

Ginger

Ethan and his grandma met us at the airport. He held his new sister in his arms and I was overwhelmed. It was a magical moment. Watching Ethan tenderly hold Olivia for the first time, I could picture them growing up together. One of the adoption prep books we read early in the process had a quiz on "Why Do You Want to Adopt?" which outlined "healthy" and "non-healthy" reasons based on how the reader answered a list of questions. According to the quiz, wanting a sibling for your child was *not* a healthy reason to adopt. But, truth be told, that was a big factor for me. Knowing Ethan's personality, I knew he would benefit from having a sibling. And seeing them together, I knew I was right!

In fact, I answered untruthfully to most of the questions: Are you trying to replace a child you lost in a miscarriage? Yes. Do you think adopting a child will solve all your problems? Yes. Are you trying to save a child from a lesser life? Yes.

Screw that quiz! Screw the experts! My reasons are mine. And I fixed what was broken and got my boy a sister. And he loves her! And we love her!

Explaining adoption to a preschooler was interesting: "Mommy and Daddy wanted to have a baby, and a woman in Ohio had a baby that grew in her tummy, but she couldn't be a mommy for the baby, and she asked us if we would be the baby's parents, *and now you are her big brother!*" Putting this complex situation into simple terms was actually a helpful exercise. And Ethan couldn't have cared less about the micro-details at that point. He was just eager to have a sibling, and loved to help bathe her, swaddle her, and go to doctor visits with her.

Lots of family and friends visited Olivia over the next couple of weeks. With all the loved ones coming together, I couldn't help but think of the extended biological family she had in Ohio she might never know and who might never know her. It was incredible how this plan had played out… that I actually brought this precious angel (yes, I still do call her that) home with me, to raise and care for forever and ever.

Our family adjusted very well. Yes, there was a transition, a "new normal" with an addition to the family, but I wonder if it would have been very different if I'd given birth to Olivia. On the other hand, it would've given Ethan some additional prep time. I quickly realized that, in those first weeks, he was still getting used to having a sibling. When Grandma came for a visit a few weeks after our homecoming, he met her at the door and exclaimed, "Grandma Colleen, the baby is still here!" *She sure is, Big Brother... she is here to stay!*

Chapter ♡ Nine
The Family Tree

A baby comes with connections. A biological mother may be in the picture or she may fade out. There may be the joy of biological siblings, who bring with them whole other sets of parents to round out your child's family—and the special delight of kin who look like your child. For Sydney, time brought with it an expanding circle of folks with roles in Cole's life, and a warm security in her own role as mother. Anticipating "family tree" projects in school, Julia found a perfect kind of tree, one that puts her child at its living heart.

Ginger

As we were setting out on the path to adoption, we learned of a local adoption facilitator who held monthly barbecues for adoptive parents and birth families, as well as those interested in adopting. Usually, a guest speaker discussed a recent placement. It sounded like a good place to mingle, share stories, and hear about some adoption successes.

At the event I had attended, a young birth mom who had just placed appeared with the adoptive parents and baby. They seemed to have a glow about them as they sat in the backyard under the redwoods explaining their story. It sounded like a fairy tale. The birth mom was in college and decided adoption was best for her baby. She felt an immediate connection with the adoptive family, had a home birth at which they were present, and even pumped to provide breast milk for the baby. I swear I thought I heard harps in the background. *These people have it all together,* I thought. No drama. They sounded so at ease, so comfortable with each other and this new extended family they had created. Could it really be that simple?

The answer: sometimes. In our case, despite many attempts, we've had no contact with Amber. For now, that door is closed. However, we've lucked out with another family connection. Our adoption attorney, Melinda, explained that Amber had two other children—a five-year-old daughter, who was living with Amber's mother, and a little boy who was eighteen months older than Olivia, whom Melinda helped place for adoption. Hearing this, I was screaming in my head, *Amber, stop having babies!* Yet at the same time, I was so thankful that she had given birth to Olivia.

Melinda asked if we would like to be connected with the adoptive parents of the little boy, Joe and Linda. Yes! We quickly jumped on a conference call. During the conversation, we realized that we had read their "Dear Birth Mother" letter during our "research," and so we felt like we already knew them. The impact was huge! They had also traveled to Ohio to briefly meet Amber after the birth of their boy, Max, who was now a happy, healthy, and lively member of their family. As an added bonus, we discovered their home was just thirty minutes away from ours, and even in that first conversation we made plans to meet when we returned to California. How amazing it felt to meet a couple who had walked in our same shoes only eighteen months prior. Within a half hour, they'd emailed us photos of their family. Everything was coming together; this connection cemented our confidence in the decision to adopt.

When Olivia was just two weeks old, Max and his family came to our home for lunch to meet our family. There was something so special about Linda and Joe's first meeting with Olivia: they already saw her as a loved one. They held her and looked into her eyes and cuddled her, saying, "Look, she and Max have the same cleft chin, the same nose." Linda and Joe were meeting a new family member. How incredible it must have been to meet your son's sister! The bond was instant. And Max's five-year-old sister, Velma, who was also placed through an open adoption, made immediate friends with our three-and-a-half-year-old son, Ethan. We knew we had grown our family.

Funny to admit, I'm not good at seeing similarities in babies—to me, a baby looks like a baby. So when Max and Olivia were young, it was hard for me to see the likeness. But as they grow older, it's remarkable how similar they look to each other: fair skin, light hair, same nose, cleft chin. A close friend who was adopted told me she always longed to see another family member who looked like her. These are the small things we take for granted in a "normal" family.

Today, we include each other in birthday celebrations and other family get-togethers. We cherish that relationship. I'm very glad Olivia will have the benefit of going through life knowing her half-brother. And we feel fortunate to have the friendly Porters as extended family. Perhaps Olivia's connection with Max will give her a sense of her roots, her history. And should she ever want to connect with Amber, perhaps Max will be her partner in the search, with both sets of adoptive parents supporting their effort. For these reasons, I am most grateful we have an open adoption.

Sydney

After Philip and I got married, the question most avoided by friends and family was about us starting a family. Nevertheless, it always came up in a roundabout way, and we sensed friends and family being sensitive to our challenges, and feeling somewhat awkward about announcing a pregnancy or talking about their own kids. When it did come out in the open, they endlessly reassured us, "Don't worry, a baby will find you." Or, "God has a plan." I couldn't imagine that being true until Cole came into our lives. Conversations about having children were so much easier and happier once we started the adoption process. And many of those conversations touched our hearts with a positive adoption story.

From the start of our marriage, I'd loved talking to Phillip about baby names. It gave me a wonderful, secure feeling to know he dreamed about our future family as I did. I had vivid memories of being a young teen and writing on a piece of paper the names of the children I was going to have when I grew up.

Never in my life did I imagine that the baby we would name someday was going to be an adopted child. He was meant to be in our life… "God's plan!"

Once we were placed with Cole, a key question for us was would Quinn feel like she was part of our family? Did we feel she was? We made it very clear that we weren't co-parenting, and what lay in the future was not necessarily an extended family but, rather, an extended relationship between Quinn and us, for Cole's sake. Quinn's mother told Quinn it was up to her to grow into the birth mom Cole would love and respect someday. I seconded that—and still do.

Our adoption attorney helped us understand that when an adoption takes place, it affects a wide-ranging collection of family members and loved ones. She helped us explore ways to honor individuals and recognize the role each person plays in the life of the adopted child. We learned to acknowledge the joy and connection as well as the more difficult emotions of grief and even loss. Yet nothing really prepared us for the overwhelming emotions we felt upon bringing a child into our home and connecting that small person with our family. Cole has a mother, father, two nanas, two papas, three aunts, four uncles, and thirteen cousins. What a blessing for him to have such a big family tree!

Elle

Harper's adoption has been very "clean" and uncomplicated. From the very first conversations I had with Rachel about her involvement in the baby's life, she repeated that I was Harper's mother and that was that, period. She explained to me that she'd been adopted when she was a day old by her adoptive parents, Deidre and Sam, and she felt these two special people who raised her were her "real" parents, not Ellen White, the woman who gave birth to her. Thankfully, for Harper's sake, Rachel was open to meeting her if and when Harper wants to meet, and she promised that I would always have her current contact information so a meeting could take place.

Then, two weeks after Harper was born, Rachel texted me with her new cell number. Two weeks later, she texted again to say she'd gone back to her old number. That text—about two-and-a-half years ago—was the last time I heard from her. At this point, we have no contact with Rachel or her immediate family. We only have her cell phone number and the address of her parents.

Julia

In our adoption parenting class, Oscar and I learned about different ways the issue of Benjamin's adoption may come up. It could happen, for example, as he looks in the mirror and sees traits different from ours: his blue eyes, his dimples. The counselors tried to prepare us to deal with several common trigger events, but one in particular struck me: inevitably Benjamin will be asked in school to create a family tree.

I began to research our options and found one particularly creative idea: instead of a typical family tree seen from the front, in which the child is one small branch within the lineage, you are looking down on the tree from above, and the child is at its center. The child is the trunk. The adoptive family's "branches" radiate from one side, the biological family's from the other. I really like this idea for many reasons. For one, it puts the emphasis on our son, since he will be at the tree's center. It also allows for more or less emphasis on the biological family. If, at that time, they are very involved, there can be several branches dedicated to that part of his lineage (biological siblings, grandparents, aunts, uncles). If not, then just a few.

Laura, Benjamin's birth mom, has two older daughters with the same father, Jonathan, both of whom she gave up for adoption. They are only eighteen months and three years older than him. As Benjamin gets older, he may want to know his full biological sisters. From the pictures we've seen, they look very much like him, and their expressions even suggest they may have similar personalities. It's possible that someday, even Oscar and I will have a relationship with Benjamin's biological sisters, and perhaps with their adoptive parents. So they may get added to the tree along with their adoptive families.

Just like a real tree, a family tree is a living thing in continual flux. There is loss and new growth. When a biological mother disappears, a no-nonsense and compassionate godmother may be heaven sent, as in Elle's case. As Ginger's family members adjusted, she heard a few well-meaning comments that tested her patience. And Julia and Sydney confronted the completely unexpected possibility of a new addition to their tree.

Ginger

There were some interesting reactions within our own families as they warmed up to embracing an adopted child. The majority of aunts, uncles, and cousins showered Olivia with love and attention. But, for a few family members, there was some adjustment: adoption had never been part of their world. When my uncle met her at three weeks old, he said, with shock, "She is perfect," as if an adopted child would have some physical defect, personality disorder, or odd smell.

Family members have also told me, clearly expecting the comment to elicit a grateful response from me, "I love her as if she were my own flesh and blood." In my head, I answer, "Of course you do! How does biology affect the level of love you give a child?"

I need to practice compassion and realize that not everyone sees through my eyes. I believe the root cause of such comments is simply inexperience, mainly evident in an older generation that held a different view of adoption.

Of course, Angelina Jolie, Sandra Bullock, and Madonna have made adoption much more mainstream. And most people are comfortable with it when viewed through the pages of *People* magazine. But it can take some adjustment when adoption leaps out of a magazine's pages and into your tight-knit family or immediate circle of friends. There was no negative intention on the part of my family members; the way I saw it, some just took a bit more time to catch up with our way of thinking.

Olivia blends into our life without any additional drama. We take pleasure in all the typical child-rearing challenges of temper tantrums, finicky eating, and potty training. (Side note: If your firstborn is adopted, you may find yourself wondering if some of the less enchanting sides of parenting are due to the adoption. *No.* Most likely, it's a one- or two-year-old acting his or her age! Breathe, it will pass.)

When we were working on our home study, our social worker, who was the adoptive parent of a girl born in China, warned that people—be they family members, friends, or even complete strangers—might make hurtful comments that could be damaging within earshot of the child. She gave us the personal example of being told more than once that her daughter was so "lucky" to have been "saved" by her adoptive parents from an inferior life in China. Certainly, this comment was made without malicious intent but, rather, gratitude for the adoptive parent creating a better life for the child. However, I understand that it did breach the boundary of personal space and might easily have been misunderstood by the child, who was then just six.

Occasionally, I will hear the comment, "Olivia is lucky to have you." My response is that *I'm* the lucky one!

Sydney

Just as we felt at peace having only one child, we got news from Quinn soon after Cole turned two that she was pregnant again, this time with twin boys! It was a bittersweet moment for me. I was moved by this extension of Cole's life. Now he had half-brothers! But I couldn't help but wonder if this was a sign that we were meant to have more than one child?

Everyone we shared the news with burst out with, "Will you adopt the twins?" As much as we wanted to know, we knew we couldn't answer the question until Quinn asked us.

During Quinn's pregnancy, I found myself wanting to connect more with her, learning as much as I could about her plans to raise or place the twins. In the end, Quinn decided she wanted to parent her twins, and Phillip and I settled back comfortably into being a one-child family. Maybe Cole will connect to his twin half-brothers later in life.

After almost three years, we've had three visits with Quinn and six with her parents, always with Cole, at nice restaurants halfway between our homes. I feel a little on edge every time we bring Cole to see any of them. But then I realize we do this for my son, and that he's too young to understand anything except that we're having lunch with friends. I know that, in time, it will get easier for me. But, for a long time, it will continue feeling like a visit with friends to Cole.

During the earliest lunch meetings, as Phillip and I shared stories about Cole—sleepless nights of feedings, diaper changes, and other newborn activities that create the first bond between baby, Mommy and Daddy—I saw so clearly that we are his parents. I always felt warm inside as we left the lunch and returned home to our family life.

Our job now, as Cole's parents, is to make sure he understands and embraces his birth story. We count our blessings every day that Cole is in our life.

I have a favorite quote that I placed on Cole's Facebook page: "If a child is born and raised in a house that is loving and nurturing, where there is complete truth about where they came from, we can't give a child a better place from which to fly."

Elle

I feel both a strong sense of loss as well as relief at having no contact with Rachel. The loss I feel is almost a form of guilt that's heightened every time I think about what Rachel is not seeing and experiencing with Harper on a daily basis, and all that I am enjoying. She brought the most incredible creature into this life and I want her to see the beauty she created and so selflessly placed in our lives. As to the relief I feel, I must admit it's quite selfish. I'm relieved to not have to deal with more "family." This is not to say that I'm against having Rachael in our lives; on the contrary, I look forward to seeing her again in the future if and when Harper wants to initiate contact with her. But, until then, according to Rachel's wishes, we'll remain respectfully quite out here on the left coast.

Jack says, "I mainly feel a sense of relief that we don't have ongoing contact with Rachel, which I believe is best for Harper. I'm thankful Rachel chose to handle our adoption the way she did: she put Harper's interests and well-being first and foremost. Her outlook was mature, thoughtful, and selfless, but I never felt any bond with her. While I'm extremely grateful for her bringing Harper into our lives, I don't feel any sense of loss or void in our lives... or Harper's. My experience is probably very different from Elle's. This was a very emotionally charged process for Elle, and she and Rachel had more frequent contact. Mine was limited to a brief phone call, a lunch discussion with her godmother, and a few minutes with her and her parents in the recovery room."

Jack continues: "I've never met my biological father, and haven't had contact with my mother since I was a teenager. I don't feel any sense of loss or absence, and have no feelings associated with being "blood relatives," a term and concept I've always thought absurd. Parenting is different than birthing, and my focus is on being a great parent to Harper."

Elle picks up the thread: "I do have a close relationship with Rachel's godmother, Nola. It was so special when Nola came to visit Harper and me at the New Jersey hotel, the week the baby was born. Truly, I am beyond lucky to have Nola in our lives. From our very first meeting when she was sent by Rachel to 'screen' a very nervous me and a cautious Jack, she immediately put both of us at ease, and we were attracted to her no-nonsense yet compassionate personality. Nola just 'gets it.'"

I look forward to the day when Harper understands who Rachel is, and is able to ask Nola any questions she has about her birth mom. Nola and I get together a few times a year and I cherish our visits. In a way, Nola has become a fairy godmother to me (and Harper), and having her as my link to Rachel feels very comforting to me..."*Thanks, Nola. You rock! Without you, Harper and I would never have found each other.*"

Julia

Soon after Benjamin turned seven months, Laura, his biological mother, wrote and asked if we could Skype her. I have to admit I was a little surprised and very nervous. What did she want? What if she saw how precious Benjamin was and wanted him back? Rational or irrational, I was on edge about it. I put it off for a few weeks until I read a post on her Facebook wall: Laura was pregnant again.

"Shocked" would be describing my reaction mildly, but I figured it was time to give her a call. Oscar and I set it up for a Saturday afternoon. Our conversation was brief but nice. She loved hearing Benjamin babble. We talked casually about the upcoming holidays, and then we brought it up: her pregnancy! She said they were excited and a little scared. We told them we were hopeful they could keep this child, and were praying for them. Then they asked us if we were thinking of adopting another child. We stumbled in our answer: "No. Uh, yes. Uh, we don't know!" Was this why she called? Was she trying to feel us out to see if we'd be interested in adopting this child? The news brought a whole new side to the idea of *open* adoption. *Open* to the rest of her babies?

We were not prepared for this. Oscar and I were always thinking about Benjamin's relationship to his older biological siblings and Oscar's children from his first marriage. We had never thought of the potential for younger ones! Oscar was not ready to adopt a second child this soon, if ever. I was struck by the idea that Benjamin could have a sibling who was his full blood, and just fifteen months younger. However, we had so recently adopted him that this was not at all on our radar. After Oscar and I discussed it and prayed on it, we decided to write Laura a letter. We told her we were hopeful and praying that this would be the time she was able to start a family. However, after speaking to her a few times, we began to understand that her desire to keep the child and the reality of her ability to do so were two separate things. There was a real possibility that she wanted us to adopt this child as well.

The idea of a second child was frightening. We felt overwhelmed by the thought. Although it would be wonderful for Benjamin to have a sibling, the addition of a second child would probably change our family drastically. Benjamin was then nine months old and an easy baby. We had a good schedule, he was sleeping through the night, and we had a part-time nanny who allowed me to work when I needed to.

How would this second child change our comfortable life with our son? For Oscar, it was a question of supporting a growing family as he passed into late middle-age and beyond. For me, it was the uncertainty, the possibility of major changes in our lives. Would it stress our marriage? Would this baby be difficult? No question we would lose more of our freedom to go out and to travel.

This potential second adoption became *another* elephant in our living room, the first having been the idea of adopting at all. I was afraid to bring it up because I knew Oscar was stressed over it. He was afraid to bring it up because he thought he would hurt my feelings. So we didn't talk about it for several months.

Both of us spent time praying about what to do. One day as I sat in the quiet of my office, I complained to God, "But it's going to be *hard!*" And He most clearly responded, "I never ask you to do things that are easy."

So that was it for me. I knew that if everything aligned—if Oscar decided in favor, and Laura placed this child—that my heart would be open.

So the tree grows, and so does the complexity of our family. Will we be a family of four? Right now I am living in uncertainty. But I am trusting in my heart and in the path God has laid before our family. He has brought us this far and I know the best is yet to come.

Chapter ♡ Ten
Baby Steps into the Future

*"Will you tell your child he or she is adopted?" That question makes
Elle, Sydney, Ginger, and Julia smile. Well, and grind their teeth
a bit.*

*Adoption has worked a miracle. Deliriously happy, all four moth-
ers are sharing this miracle with their children at an early age.
Sydney found the perfect book to help her do this with Cole. Ginger conveys the good news to Olivia through a loving retelling
of her story—so familiar to her now, it's no big deal, and that's
just what Mommy wants. Elle is adamant there will never be a*

jarring "talk" that stuns Harper with the news of her adoption. Julia will encourage Benjamin to make the global journeys she and Oscar have had, so he sees how rich he is in the things that matter. With a strong sense of being loved, chosen, and precious to their families, these four youngsters are well equipped to meet life with confidence and security... perhaps even more than the average child.

Julia

Before we had Benjamin, I made a resolution that I would stop going to a particular friend's parties. They were always attended by "mommies" who talked endlessly about their baby's nursing habits, pooping styles, playtime, sleeptime, their pregnancies... on and on and on. Usually, I got stuck in the middle of the conversation with nothing to say and no way to escape. I was trapped in the misery of listening to stories about things I thought I'd never experience. So I quit socializing in that circle. It was easy to feel sorry for myself there. I'd often think, *If these women only knew how easy they have it. How unfair my life is. How they don't have to cope with anything hard like infertility.* Self-pity and even anger came easily. But the world isn't a fair place; I know that.

Oscar and I have been involved in international missions for several years. He worked abroad for over twenty years before we met and, during that time, he traveled to the poorest of poor nations. He helped bring water systems, hospitals, schools, and orphanages to those who didn't have the opportunities and resources that we do. I've had the privilege of joining him on several trips since we've been married. In places like India and Nepal, Honduras and the Philippines, we've seen and met people who have nothing: no water, no food, no family, no home. In places like these, when my soft bed and warm shower are thousands of miles away, I realize what I *do* have, and what I so often take for granted.

Back home, I struggled daily with why I couldn't have children and why everyone else appeared to have such a perfect life. But gaining knowledge of the lives of others, in places where they are far less fortunate than I am, changed me. My First World problems were nothing in light of those in the Third World. So how will this experience help Benjamin cope positively with being adopted? *I discovered that how you respond to your life's circumstances is mostly a matter of perspective.*

From the beginning, Oscar and I plan on talking to Benjamin about how we wanted him as our son so badly and for so long. When we look at pictures of Laura, or talk about her, we'll tell him he came from her tummy right into our hearts. I think that will suffice for his first few years, but I'm certain that, as he gets older and matures, there will be more questions. Harder issues. Maybe even heartbreak and anger. It's difficult to imagine how I would react if I were adopted, but I think the hurt may be similar to what I felt at those parties: he may feel like he doesn't belong, or that "everyone else" gets to experience things that he never will. We hope that his perspective on being adopted won't be one of anger or self-pity, but one of understanding and gratefulness. Life's opportunities are wide open for Benjamin. It is in these opportunities that we hope he learns *perspective* is what matters in understanding his past, as well as in pursuing his future.

It is our hope that Benjamin will be able to experience the kind of eye-opening journeys that his father and I have. Through these experiences, he'll see the world, serve others, and come to feel that, even though his life hasn't been fair in every way, he has much to be thankful for: a birth mother who loved him enough to place him for adoption when she knew she couldn't parent him; and a mother and father who desired and longed to raise him as their beloved son.

We hope his perspective on being adopted won't be one of anger or self-pity, but one of understanding and gratefulness. Life's opportunities are wide open for Benjamin.

Sydney

It's almost hard to believe Cole has been in our life longer than the process of starting our family. Every so often, I realize with surprise and a smile that the long-lingering question, "Will we ever have a family?" no longer crosses my mind with its old power to bring tears.

Every day gives us more of an established role in Cole's life as his mother and father, and confirms to us that our wait was meant to be, and that he is worth every tearful letdown in our many attempts to have a child.

Frankly, these days, we don't think about adoption as much as we did the first year. We're simply too busy being parents, worrying about getting Cole off the bottle or thinking about potty training at the right age!

We continue to hope our visits with Quinn will strengthen her happiness about all we can offer Cole, and lessen the void she might still hold in her heart. We have the joy of a child who is beyond what we imagined. We recognize we're lucky to be in a position to raise him in a healthy and secure environment, full of life adventures. We think back on the day Cole came into our life and feel so grateful we were there to welcome him into the world. And we reflect often on what life would be like without him. Just like most parents, we wonder what on earth we did with our time before our son, and what could possibly have brought us any greater joy.

We share with as many people as possible how positive the adoption journey has been for us. And we know we're not alone in the once-lonely world of adoption. We are part of something that's growing much more common today.

We anticipate the day Cole understands his wonderful adoption story as we share it with him. What questions will he ask? How much will it really matter to him? I'm reassured by the thought that, by the time Cole fully understands what adoption means, he'll have met more kids who know they've been adopted than he might have even a decade ago. These experiences will help him talk openly with us about his own adoption.

We were given many children's books about adoption, and have read one in particular over and over to Cole: Tell Me Again about the Night I Was Born. The book is written in the voice of a child asking his parents to tell him a story about his birth, and what it was like for them. The child asks, "Tell me again how you got the call in the middle of the night and they told you I was born." At this point, I always tell Cole how excited I felt when we got the call that we'd been chosen to be his parents. I know that, at age two, this is barely making sense! But hearing it over and over will make the details familiar, comfortable, and more normal. It will also encourage Cole to ask questions, just as the child does in the story.

At an adoption workshop, I was told that, in the end, Cole will be the one to decide if he wants to share with others that he was adopted. We have a calm faith that we'll deal successfully as a family with all these questions and answers as we journey through Cole's life with him.

One of the best things I did to cherish and share our adoption journey with Cole was to create an Adoption Book rather than a Baby Book. Complete with photos and quotes that inspired us during the times of uncertainty, it fully reveals the beautiful journey that brought him into our life.

After a few years of parenting Cole, we realize adoption is just as much a blessing for us as it is for him. The day Cole fully understands who gave birth to him is a day we hope fills his heart with more love for his birth mom and the wise and brave choice she made for him. We hope he values us for choosing open adoption and celebrates that we were chosen to be his parents. We will help him grow to understand how special open adoption is, and how it means he won't have to live a life darkened by mysteries and secrets. We believe that honesty about his birth story will give Cole a secure feeling about who he is, which is the best thing parents can give a child.

Ginger

I tell both my kids they are "unique recipes, never to be duplicated." I explain to them that my sister and I have the same mom and dad, and that Daddy has three sisters and brothers from the same parents. But *my* kids have a birth mom/dad combo that, unless there is some bizarre act of nature, will never be duplicated. This makes them special!

Each one has a unique story, and I retell it to them often, usually at bedtime.

Like most kids (adopted or biological), Olivia loves hearing her birth story, especially when the telling is accompanied by looking at photos of herself as a baby—when I first met her at twelve hours old, when Daddy held her for the first time four days later, and her first photo with her brother and other family members.

When I tell Olivia her "special story," I describe our wishing for a baby for years, getting an amazing phone call, rushing out to meet her, falling in love with her, and bringing her home to live with our family. I explain that I had hoped and prayed for a little girl… I even named her years before… and, finally, my prayers were answered!

Olivia listens closely, and is very attentive to each detail. I usually hug her at the end, saying, "We brought you home to be part of our family forever and ever!" And I tell her that her mom and dad and brother love her, and all her grandparents, aunts, uncles, and cousins love her. She is loved! By now, Olivia has heard it often enough to recite parts of the story to me. Perhaps her reaction will change as she matures but, for now, her response is a combination of positive with an "It's no big deal" attitude. After hearing the story, her typical next move is to ask, "Can I have more mac and cheese?" As if to say, you love me and I love you, and that is what matters. She has taught me so much!

It's interesting to occasionally hear questions like, "What are your plans for helping your child cope in the most positive way with being adopted?" The question makes it sound like we're dealing with a tragedy of some sort. Yes, there is some sadness for the biological family with whom Olivia may never have a relationship. But we have presented it as this: Amber loved Olivia so much that she wanted to give her the best life possible. Our decision is to be open and honest about our amazingly positive adoption experience. Olivia has a great story, one she can be proud of.

We have it easier than some, as Olivia's looks are not strikingly different from her brother Ethan's, so most people are surprised to learn that she is adopted. I joke with friends that I got an adoption form and checked the boxes for a blonde, blue-eyed, fair-skinned baby girl. I'm sure it would be different if we had a child of a different race. However, in our case, her adoption is not physically obvious. *It is also not a secret.* It is something we share but don't broadcast.

Olivia is growing up knowing she joined our family through the miracle of adoption. It will always be part of her world. Because she is only three, many of

126

the tougher questions have not been asked at this point—she doesn't even know where babies come from yet. Some of these questions might surface as she gets older and realizes her story is different from most of her friends. We're preparing for that now. I'm already explaining to her that there are many ways to create a family and that lots of families have unique situations, like two mommies or two daddies.

I hope to always have an open relationship with Olivia, one in which she knows I welcome her questions and she feels she can speak freely about her feelings with us. Will she, at some point, feel abandoned by her biological parents? Will she feel disconnected from our family as an adopted member? Perhaps she'll have these feelings as she nears the teenage years, when many kids can struggle with identity issues. I'm already preparing for the day when she's in middle school and, during an argument, throws at me the words, "You're not even my real mom!" I'm practicing a couple of responses along the lines of, "Biology does not make a family.... love does."

Elle

More often than I can even keep track of, I've been asked this question, usually delivered in a rushed whisper from family and friends: "So how will you explain to Harper that she is adopted?"

This was, in fact, the same question I anxiously pondered during my Virgin America flight from San Francisco to New York, where I could be "ringside" in the days before Rachel gave birth. While I waited to be called to the hospital, I mentally duked it out in my head: "So, Elle, how and when will you tell this baby that she was adopted, and how can you assure her that she wasn't abandoned or given up but, in fact, that she has been given the purest form of love… selfless love given from Rachel to her for a bigger and better life?"

I honestly couldn't find an answer to this question then. But once I met my daughter that early spring morning in mid-May at the hospital, just minutes after she was born, I can honestly say that this question never popped into my head again. *As soon as I laid eyes on her, I knew she was my daughter and I was her mother.*

Harper's birth story and how she came to us through the path of adoption is the most incredible story I will ever share with anyone on this earth. As she grows up, and repeatedly listens to, and begins to comprehend the magic of what I feel toward her—the sheer odds of us finding each other—she will understand how much Jack and I love her. She will know how unbelievably lucky we feel to have been given the privilege of parenting her and calling her our daughter.

Harper will know she is our daughter who came to us through the amazing journey of adoption, a path Jack and I wholeheartedly chose, and that this path was not chosen by default; it was chosen with strong intention and with the purest form of love. There will never be a "day" when Harper suddenly learns she is adopted. Because since that first life-changing morning when we met her just minutes after she was born, I've been sharing and celebrating with her and others the incredible journey Jack and I took to find her, and how once we found her. She completed our family, bringing life, love, and magic into our hearts and our home.

Of course, Harper doesn't understand what I've been sharing with others while cradling her in my arms or bouncing her on my hip. But the point I want to make crystal-clear is that her arrival in our family through adoption has not been some secret I tell others behind closed doors, or otherwise out of Harper's earshot. Actually, it's quite the opposite. Harper has been right there with me, at my side, as I've proudly shared *our* birth story and tried to show others what a healthy adoption can look like.

Far too many times, after I've openly and honestly shared with others how she came into our family, I've had ignorant or insensitive comments thrown my way. I do my best to stay calm and to regard the exchange as an education for my questioner. But, OMG, it can be tough. Here are a few of my all-time "favorite" questions:

Question #1: "Oh, I am sooo sorry [that you had to adopt]. Do you have any children of your own?" (I was asked this question just recently at the gym in Harper's daycare center. I seriously wanted to punch the girl in the face, but she was just young and naïve.)

My Answer: "Yes, I have child of my own, her name is Harper. In fact, you happen to be holding her right now."

This same young and naïve woman followed up with my favorite Question #2: "What country is she from, and how old was she when you got her?"

My Answer: "She was born in the United States of America in a faraway place called New Jersey and was, oh, about five minutes young when I met her."

Young Naïve Girl: "You mean you can still adopt within the United States?" (Yes, this exchange happened.)

Question #3: "Now that you've adopted, you know you'll finally get pregnant, don't you? Women who adopt always end up getting pregnant."

My Answer: "First off, are you implying that the adoption won't have any meaning if I then get pregnant? Second off, adoption is not a 'fertility treatment' or a 'chill pill' that helps you get pregnant. In fact, fewer than five percent of people who adopt become pregnant without trying."

Question: "Doesn't it worry you that you don't know what you're 'in for' with your adopted child?"

My Answer: "No. It's not as if I'd know what I was 'in for' if I had a biological baby, either."

And my all-time "favorite":
Question: "Will you tell your daughter that she is adopted?"

My Answer: "Ummm, is this a trick question? Of course!"

And now, here's a few more "favorite" comments I've been offered:
—"Your daughter looks like she could be yours!" (The reply in my head: *Well, guess what? She is mine....she's all mine. And, yes, I agree with you that she looks similar to me; gosh am I lucky, because she is damn gorgeous. Thank you for the compliment.*)

—"Too bad you had to adopt, your real kids would have been really cute."

—"Why didn't you just have your own kids?"

—"Can they [her birthparents] get her back?"

And the one that totally takes the cake, (drum roll, please)…

—"Can you give her back if you find there's something wrong with her?"

Jack and I will begin to share her adoption story with Harper when the time is right. This will probably occur in the next year or so, as she enters pre-school and becomes able to understand that "Mommy's tummy could not grow a baby, but the tummy of another young and brave woman named Rachel *could* grow a baby. Rachel, your very beautiful and kind birth mommy, grew you in her tummy, but was too young to take care of you all by herself. Rachel was very smart and knew that she had to find a very special family to take care of you better than she could. She searched high and low to find the perfect family who would take the best care of you because you are *so* special to her. And, guess what? She found us… Daddy and me! Your Daddy and I love you more than anything in this world. *You are a baby who was born in both of our hearts, just not in my tummy.* We will always be a part of each other, and even after you grow up, you will always live in our hearts. Always."

As Harper grows in her ability to understand, we'll share with her how excited we were when we traveled back east to be there to meet her in the hospital when she was born, and how it felt to first see her and hold her and kiss her and hug her. I'll share with her the details of her first diaper change and the first bottle she drank, and the cool fact that Jack and I, together, fed her that first bottle. I will proudly share with her that every nurse we spoke with in the hospital those first few days took us aside and told us that she was the most beautiful newborn they had ever laid eyes on.

I will giddily speak of our first night together as a family back at the hotel in Jersey City and how I didn't sleep a wink because I was too busy memorizing her breathtaking face and listening to her soft newborn coos and breathing. I will share with her how we treated her like fine china as we cautiously made our way through the airport to make our first-class flight back home to San Francisco (starting at just nine days old… nothing but the best for our baby girl).

I'm hopeful Harper will react positively when she starts to hear her magical story. But, of course, there's no guarantee. All we can do is be truthful and honest and continually reassure her that she is the most incredible gift we have ever been given and will ever receive.

It's when she reaches middle childhood, when I won't always be there with her to navigate and educate others on the topic of adoption, that she may be exposed to some of society's negative views of adoption. Negative and naïve comments, intentional or not, may come from strangers, schoolmates, family and, for damn sure, the media. I am prepared and ready for these incidents, and I will passionately continue to be an adoption advocate/educator in my community. I will use these potentially hurtful encounters as opportunities to explain to Harper and reassure her that the curiosity she and others feel about adoption is not only healthy, but productive, and that I welcome all questions she, her friends, teachers, or our family may have about her and our family's birth story. I will always make sure Harper feels comfortable asking any questions she might have or expressing any fears she may experience.

A few days after Harper was born, I saw the most inspirational poster on the wall at HAPS, the placement agency we worked with. It captures what I will express and share with Harper when she's old enough to understand its meaning...

Dear ♡ Child

The Legacy of an Adopted Child

Once there were two women who never really knew each other . . .

One, you do not remember. The other, you call Mother.

Two different lives shaped to make you one.

One became your guiding star. The other became your sun.

The first one gave you life and the second taught you to live it.

The first gave you a need for love. The second was there to give it.

One gave you a nationality. The other gave you a name.

One gave you a talent. The other gave you aim.

One gave you emotions. The other calmed your fears.

One saw your first sweet smile. The other dried your tears.

One sought a home for you that she could not provide.

The other prayed for a child and her hope was not denied.

And now you ask me through your tears the age-old question—unanswered
  throughout the years— is it heredity or environment? Which are you a
  part of?

Neither, my darling, neither.

Just two different kinds of love.

—Author Unknown

Epilogue
Circle of Friends

Now, we've told you the stories of our adoption journeys. But there's another story left untold: the story we four marvel at whenever we're together. It's the tale of how we all met, how our friendships affected our four very different adoption journeys, and how we feel about writing this book together. We thought you might be curious to know. Of course, to tell this story, we must go back in time a good many years.

Sydney and Phillip dated off and on for twenty years before marrying. So, naturally, Sydney knew Phillip's good buddy, Gordon. The two men were friends since high school, and had been roommates after college while living in San Francisco. When Gordon married Ginger, Phillip and Sydney were "on" again—this time, with a new sense of commitment. Sydney and Ginger met at Gordon's fortieth birthday party in the summer of 2003. Ginger says, "I instantly fell in love with Sydney! She was warm, genuine and fun."

The two women became good friends, sharing with each other their intense desire to start a family. But Ginger wasn't sharing everything; she was private about her and Gordon's infertility challenges. Over time, however, it became too obvious to keep secret from Sydney and Phillip. Recalls Sydney: "We'd have vacations scheduled and, out of nowhere, Gordon and Ginger would have to change dates and plans. Finally Ginger opened up to me, and Gordon opened up to Phillip, that they were doing IVF, and their lives had to revolve around doctor appointments and planned transfers."

Once Sydney and Phillip realized what Gordon and Ginger were going through, they wondered about their own ability to have children. Both in their forties, they began having "baby-making sex" even before marrying, to test the waters. It didn't work, either before or after they married.

Then, after many IVF attempts, Ginger and Gordon got pregnant using a donor egg. They were over the moon. Soon, Sydney and Phillip were enjoying family trips with Ginger, Gordon, and baby Ethan. The two women had fun thinking about having babies together—Ginger's second and Sydney's first.

It wasn't until Ginger got stuck on having baby number two that Sydney began to panic about making her own baby number one. Little did she and Phillip know, they would end up following Ginger and Gordon all the way through many more IVFs (and, in their case, trying repeatedly with a surrogate), then giving up, as their friends had, to go the route of adopting.

Ginger and Gordon were already placed with their daughter, Olivia, when Sydney and Phillip did yet another IVF transfer with a surrogate. The protocol was forty-eight hours of bed rest for the surrogate. They asked Emma where she'd like hang out while resting, and she picked a quaint little B&B just outside San Francisco.

After checking in, Sydney, Phillip, Emma in pajamas, and her husband, Blake, all celebrated the latest transfer with a toast at the inn's wine and cheese hour. A couple approached the group, apparently from out of town, asking for tips on good places to dine in town. It was Julia and Oscar. Sydney and Phillip recommended their favorite local eateries and, as Oscar and Julia drifted off, the foursome laughed at Blake's murmured comment, "I bet they're trying to figure out *our* story."

By chance—although Sydney maintains that nothing about this meeting was coincidence, that it was meant to be—they all ended up at the same restaurant, and Sydney and Phillip invited Julia and Oscar to their table. As introductions went around again, out popped the loaded question. "Where's Emma?" Julia asked innocently. As Sydney remembers it, "Blake, Phillip, and I all stared blankly at each other, and finally one of us said she wasn't feeling well and had stayed at the hotel to rest. We dodged that question easily, but not the next one. Julia asked, "How do you all know each other?" This was a funny and awkward moment, and I'm not sure who if not all of us at once blurted out, "They—we—we're having their—a—baby!" It was so jumbled we had to go on to explain. But that awkward moment turned into moments of truth and trust, with people we then called strangers and now call friends.

Julia and Oscar, who live in Colorado, were visiting Oscar's family in California for Thanksgiving. They'd come to the B&B for some time alone. Says Sydney of that fateful encounter, "In one night, we four became connected with the common challenge of infertility. Julia and Oscar shared so many personal and heartbreaking stories about their quest to have a baby. They left wanting to stay in touch and made us promise to let them know how it worked out with our surrogate."

Julia adds, "We didn't know it when we checked into the inn, but the weekend we spent there would change everything for us. We met Sydney and Phillip, and discovered the commonality that would impact the rest of our lives: infertility. The encounter, and the developing friendship that led us to the path of adoption, had an incredibly positive result. Most people spend a romantic weekend together and end up with a baby in nine months. Oscar and I spent the weekend together… and ended up with a baby two-and-a-half years later!"

As positive as their meeting was, the negative came when Sydney had to tell Julia and Oscar that their transfer hadn't taken. As agreed by Sydney and Phillip beforehand, this failure marked the end of the surrogate road for them. They now looked with hopefulness to adoption.

Sydney says, "Julia and I were placed in each other's paths that evening to create the same connection I had with Ginger. Only now it was *our* turn to lead the way." For Julia and Oscar would soon follow them on the path to adoption, just as Sydney and Phillip had followed Ginger and Gordon.

Julia puts it this way: "The biggest blessing for us in knowing Sydney and Phillip has been their encouragement. Through their example, their endless advice, and their friendship, we gained the confidence to adopt. Once we were on the path, they reassured us through difficult times of waiting, and celebrated with us when we reached our goal."

While Sydney endured the difficult wait for a birth mom match, her friend visiting from Australia was a welcome distraction. One morning, they planned a fun time shopping local stores. Sydney wanted to introduce Marie to San Francisco shops that were one-of-a-kind. And she knew just the one: a chic boutique owned by a friend of a friend. But when they arrived at the store in a downpour, it was closed. Sydney remembers: "A note on the door said the owner was closing the store to start a new path in life."

Call the next twist a coincidence… or another example of a connection that was meant to be. Sydney was so curious about the intriguing message she called the friend who knew the owner. "What was up?" Much to Sydney's surprise, her friend told her that Elle and her husband, Jack, were starting their family through adoption, and that they'd just got the call to pick up their baby girl.

"What?" Sydney says. "Was this a sign? Everyone around me was abuzz about adoption, and now this retail dynamo, too?" Sydney asked her friend if she thought Elle would be okay with contacting her to learn about her adoption process. The upshot was Elle's number in her hand. Though eager for details, she decided to wait and give the new mother time to settle in with her baby. She would reach out to her when she and Phillip were placed too. Three months later, Cole came into their lives. It was the perfect time to connect with Elle.

Things happened fast. No sooner did Sydney email Elle with well wishes for her adopted baby girl, also sharing the news of her own adopted baby boy, then the two made a lunch date. "From that point on," Sydney says, "we were bonded by the beauty of these babies, and found ourselves crying over the same emotions. We, too, were meant to be connected by the journey of adoption."

Soon after, Sydney brought Elle and Ginger together. The two bonded instantly. The setting was heavenly: a Caribbean vacation on a boat with Sydney and Phillip. Elle remembers, "Deep at sea, with crystal-blue waters and skies enveloping us, Ginger and I shared our adoption journeys. We laughed… and cried." Ginger adds, "As Elle and I walked on the beach, talking about our baby-making efforts, we found so many similarities in situations and feelings. One big one was experiencing the hurt inside after another failed IVF cycle, but having to appear like all is well to family and friends who continued to pop out the kids with no effort. Sometimes it helps just to know someone else has walked in those shoes."

Meanwhile, Sydney kept everyone up to date on Julia, Oscar, and their adopted son, Benjamin. Then, in April 2013, all four couples, children in tow, met at a dinner party at Sydney and Phillip's home. That enchanted evening Julia, Oscar, and Benjamin were taken to everyone's hearts in a nanosecond.

This was no ordinary gathering. For these relationships were like none other in their lives. "No one got it like the people in this room." Says Ginger, "Throughout the family-building process, I often felt no one understood me. How could I smile and feel happy and go to work and be expected to live a normal life with this infertility cloud over my head? These friends had been through it."

For Elle, writing the book captures that special understanding, and she offers it to others. "I have openly shared with my closest friends and family the roller coaster ride of unique experiences one goes through on the journey of adoption. And yet I do not feel *completely* understood by them. This is not the case with Sydney, Ginger, and Julia. I feel completely understood by these women. This special understanding doesn't even have to be put into words. And it has been so comforting and so healing for me... and, I hope, for others who read this book."

Julia also hopes to help others through the book. In fact, she already has. "I've already had the chance to share my experience with several women struggling with infertility. And I feel my sharing so openly helped them. I feel the book will not only broaden our audience, but also increase our credibility. When I tell people I'm helping to write this book, they feel more open about asking questions about my journey. Thanks to the book, I'm hoping many more people will be able to take something from my experience and apply it in a helpful way to their own journey."

Says Sydney of her motives for being the guiding force in pulling the four journeys together, "We knew we had a story to share and document for ourselves, others seeking adoption, and our children."

"I often wish," muses Ginger, "that *I'd* had a book like this when I started the adoption process. It's so special hearing from people who have traveled the journey and been successful. It helps take the mystery and fear out of the experience." She continues, "It's not like it's written by someone with a sociology degree, and it's not a clinical study with a lot of percentages. It's totally raw and real... real-life stories spoken from the heart. When we four started out, we heard the experts, and we followed some advice and didn't follow some. But this book is on a whole different level: it's about the experience itself. I'm not sure there's anything like it. I'm so glad we're putting it out there to help others."

Ginger adds, "Because our personalities, styles, and experiences are so different, the reader will probably identify with one of us. She'll go, 'That's totally me! I went through that exact same thing!'"

For all these reasons, Sydney, Elle, Julia, and Ginger wrote this book... for *you*.

www.ingramcontent.com/pod-product-compliance
Lightning Source LLC
Chambersburg PA
CBHW070044100426
42740CB00013B/2784